LB 1050.5 .T85 1998

Tuley, Ann Cashwell.

Never too late to read

D0206275

DATE DUE

BRODART, CO.   Cat. No. 23-221-003

NEVER TOO LATE
TO READ

Language Skills for the Adolescent with Dyslexia

Based on the Work of Alice Ansara

Ann Cashwell Tuley

York Press, Inc.
Baltimore, Maryland

Copyright 1998 by York Press

All rights reserved including the right to reproduce this book or por-tions thereof in any form except for the inclusion of brief quotations in a review. All inquiries should be addressed to York Press, Inc., P.O. Box 504, Timonium, Maryland 21094.

The book was manufactured in the United States of America.
Typography by Type Shoppe II Productions, Ltd.
Printing and binding by P. A. Hutchison Company
Cover Design by Joseph Dieter, Jr.

Tuley, Ann Cashwell.
    Never too late to read : language skills for the adolecent with
dyslexia : based on the work of Alice Ansara / Ann Cashwell Tuley.
        p.   cm.
    Includes bibliographical references (p.) and index.
    ISBN 0-912752-47-5
    1. Reading--Remedial teaching. 2. Language arts--Remedial
teaching. 3. Dyslexic children--Educaton. 4. Ansara, Alice.
I. Title.
LB1050.5.T85 1998
371.91'44--dc21   98-45948
                                                            CIP

DEDICATION

To my children and the anonymous sixteen-year-old LD student who wrote the following:

My life is not going so good rite now and I dont know waet to do so I feel like the only thing to do is to kill my self and I will be a lot deder than now so the frist thing is I have the read bad cold and it waint leve and the second thing is my gir friend went back to Johnny 3 day agow and I gust don't know wait to do rite now and another thing is school. I need som help and so plece someone help me

Contents

ACKNOWLEDGMENTS

Some of Alice Ansara's most valuable insights were conveyed to her students. A special thanks to Constance Dwyer Porter, Martie Torza, Harley Tomey, III, Rebecca Richardson, and Lois Wolf for sharing classnotes and information: and to Aaron Tuley for technical assistance. Also, a note of appreciation for the dedicated and enormously helpful work of Carolyn Bowen, Mary Cheatham and Ruth Lund, Aylett Cox, Lida Helson, Mildred Plunkett, Elsie Rak, and Beth Slingerland.

Foreword

I am not sure exactly when or how Alice Ansara and I met, but in a very short time we carried on animated talks on the reading field, the latest research, and what would and would not work.

In my advanced course on reading difficulties at the Harvard Graduate School of Education, various researchers, scholars, and clinicians were invited to discuss their work. Alice came to do so several times. She was most stimulating and shared with us her mode of practice that was successful with adolescents who had dyslexia.

Her lectures were exciting and inspiring. She brought us the best of what she knew from research and theory. In addition, she brought her own clinical insights and workable suggestions for practice.

Never Too Late to Read is based on her broad knowledge of learning disabilities, and particularly the clinical practice that she brought to bear on the reading difficulties of adolescents. It focuses on adolescents who read poorly within the full ranges of development—from those beginning to read to those who are quite advanced. The book, therefore, is useful, not only for adolescents, but for those on lower levels of reading ability—those still in elementary and middle schools.

It is remarkable how much Alice Ansara was ahead of her time. She anticipated the findings from research on the importance of using reading materials that are not too easy. She advised teachers to be cautious about following the then current practice of selecting "high interest, low vocabulary" reading materials. The adolescent with dyslexia, she said, needs instead a more difficult vocabulary, rich language, and high literary content. She recommended that "developmental levels should always be considered as many adolescents are quite able to grasp more abstract patterns of thought. If taught to use his cognitive skills, his strengths, and his acquired knowledge, the adolescent is able to make faster progress than a young child."

Since she gave this advice, two research studies have confirmed it—in a 1977 study of the reading difficulty of textbooks related to SAT scores, I found (with Susan Harris Sharples and Sue Conard) that reading harder books led to higher SAT scores than reading easier books. Hayes, Wolfer and Wolfe confirmed these findings in 1993.

Ansara suggested that teachers form a partnership with students. This is pursued from the beginning diagnosis, where results, including items the student has misread, are discussed with the student.

The teaching suggestions are useful, not only for students with reading problems, but generally. Ansara started with the importance of seeking the help of guidance counselors, administrators, and student's other teachers in order to reverse the adolescent's helplessness about his or her problem. "They need to be convinced that if they are able to develop the appropriate skills and language they can be successful."

She urged teachers to be frank with students that the needed instruction will take time and that sometimes it will be boring.

Ansara believed that teachers of adolescents with dyslexia must work at two levels at the same time—one level is teaching the techniques to enable the student to meet the requirements of his current academic classes. The other level is the language training designed to help the student overcome his deficit.

A characteristic of her approach was to bring her adolescents with dyslexia to a more mature level than is done in most remedial programs. She worked on fluency, on phrasing, and on signal words—words that signal meaning, e.g., *but, for, because, still, however, since.*

One of her "mature" techniques was the use of "penciling" to develop fluency, to overcome insertions and omissions, to recognize syllables and affixes, and to identify key words and phrases for reading comprehension.

She also suggested developing the student's ability to use textbooks through an understanding of how they are organized, where information can be found, and how to use a dictionary and take notes.

Intermingled with insights in teaching reading, Ansara advised teachers to attend to the adolescent as a person and as a student needing sensitive, structured instruction.

This book contains materials from which the teacher can develop exercises in phonics, spelling, and phrasing. It also provides lists of words that follow certain spelling rules—words that are very well known but often escape us when we try to explain to students why certain words are pronounced and spelled a certain way.

Ansara's book is what the reading field is seeking today—a wise and balanced approach to teaching reading. It is a treasure.

Jeanne S. Chall
Harvard University

References

Chall, J. S., Conard, S. S., and Harris, S. H. 1977. An Analysis of textbooks in relation to declining SAT scores. Prepared for the Advisory Panel on the Scholastic Aptitude Test Score Decline, jointly sponsored by the College Board and Educational Testing Service.

Hayes, D., Wolfer, L., and Wolfe, M. 1993, August. Was the decline in SAT-verbal scores caused by simplified school texts? Paper presented at the annual meeting of the American Sociological Association, Miami Beach, FL.

Preface

The late Alice Ansara, a unique and talented teacher, scholar, writer, and consultant, had many insights into the educational process. She was aware of the impact advancing technology, dislocated urban populations, fragmented families, and sudden and unresearched shifts in educational methods and curriculum have on schools. The problem of reading difficulties, however, and the resultant high incidence of semi-illiterate graduates, school dropouts, and juvenile delinquents were topics of primary concern. The plight of the adolescent with dyslexia, which she referred to in a speech (date unknown) as a "grim tale of absolute neglect and lack of understanding," became the focus of her teaching and writing.

Ansara noted in the same speech that at one of the most "crucial periods of his life, when he is undergoing rapid physiological and psychological changes, the adolescent with Specific Language Disability (SLD) finds himself in an academic setting far different from elementary school and placed with subject teachers who have had little training in the recognition of language disability." In addition, Ansara believed that the problem of dyslexia or SLD, compounded by a proliferation of terms and teacher expectations that it is "too late" to save these students, also contribute to feelings of frustration and failure (1972a).

In order to evaluate and remediate students with language problems, Ansara thought it essential that teachers have some background knowledge of language acquisition and maturational development. They must also know how to discuss goals and expectations with students, to select appropriate tests, and to use test results as useful prompts for teaching and for setting goals. Teachers must be able to prepare programs of reading and writing instruction, and provide learning in small sequential steps. They must allow students with dyslexia more time to respond and more time on task than other students. In addition, teachers must remember that they are not teaching programs but individuals, who are not bundles of deficits but whole human beings.

To salvage the language potential of adolescents with dyslexia, Ansara proposed a two-level approach: to teach students the study skills necessary for academic survival and to re-mediate language deficits. However, these two areas can be integrated. Dictionary use, for example, should be taught with vocabulary, and many vocabulary words obtained from the student's textbooks. For overcoming reading difficulties, Ansara urged teachers to use multisensory techniques, such as pencil-ing and simultaneous oral spelling (S.O.S.), based on a language sequence developed by Samuel Orton, Anna Gillingham, and Bessie Stillman. She also thought it essential that students keep a language notebook containing dictation, lists, and passages for readings, study skills, and all that they learn about the sound, structure, and meaning of the English language.

One of Ansara's most important contributions was her emphasis on signal words and phrasing, which she considered the most neglected keys to reading comprehension. Although many teachers believe that when a student is able to decode words with ease, the most important work is done, Ansara maintained that until students are adept at phrasing, anticipating thought, and understanding the important functions of signal words, they will probably continue reading in a word-by-word manner.

In addition to her techniques and concerns about reading, one cannot help but believe that if Ansara were alive today, she would have grasped the implications of computer technology in the classroom, devising programs for phonics, syllabication, and other aspects of language remediation. Such technological support enables teachers, too often constrained by time and large classes, to individualize instruction more easily. Although teaching, presumably, would still occur in such technologically ori-ented classrooms, students would be working together in smaller groups, problem-solving as teams and as individuals, guided and monitored by the teacher (Kaufman 1997).

Finally, Ansara urged all teachers to be aware that

> ... if we can come to recognize that in any given classroom,
> in public or independent schools, we will have extreme
> variation among children—in convergent and divergent
> thinking, in oral and written language, in problem identifi-
> cation and solving, in degree of initiative, in aggression and
> passivity, in perception and imagination, in empathy and
> apathy, in physical strength and energy, in ego strength
> and dependency, in the arts and in the mechanics—if we
> can see these things, then we will also see that there are no
> exceptional children, only different children, each with cer-
> tain needs (1979).

The book that Alice Ansara had wanted to assemble from
her various writings for teachers, tutors, parents, and all those
concerned with the fate of adolescents with dyslexia, was delayed by her death; but Ansara's approach to language, her
techniques, her concern for the uniqueness of every child, are as
valuable and as needed today as they were years ago.

Chapter 1

The Adolescent with Dyslexia

By the time they reach adolescence, many students with developmental reading disability or dyslexia, have already developed patterns of avoidance, denial, and resistance that make the teacher's task complex and difficult. After many years of academic failure, these students may have already given up hope of continuing their education or training. As Alice Ansara observed, such students are often misunderstood, mislabeled, and considered unmotivated and without goals, while the real problem is ignored and neglected. She described the vulnerability of these particular students during the bewildering years of adolescence, when discouragement and self-hatred cause many of them to drop out of school (1972a). Therefore, and this point cannot be overly stressed, if these students are to become successful adults, their language problems must be addressed. For many of these students, middle school or junior high and high school represent the last opportunity for salvaging their learning potential.

In a comprehensive study of literacy, Kirsh et al. (1993) found that 40 to 44 million Americans cannot perform elementary reading tasks such as finding information in short news articles or writing their names on forms. Many of this population are unable to earn a satisfactory living or to be productive in our society. In another study of inner-city adults with severe reading difficulties, Gottesman et al. (1996) found that the majority of these adults had developmental reading disorders, were unemployed, suffered from health problems and substance abuse, and had emotional problems such as depression, lowered self-esteem, sadness, and frustration. Most needed economic assistance. The lower the reading skill, the more severe were social and economic consequences, and the need not only for reading therapy but for a variety of social services. Thus, it is clear that unless the language problems of many adolescents are recognized and remediated, the future for most of these young people, even the brightest, may be personal and economic disaster.

In a longitudinal study concerning the prevalence of reading problems among school children, Shaywitz and colleagues (1990) concluded that one of every seven elementary school children in the United States has a reading problem. And, although there are many reasons for poor reading skills—maturational delay, faulty vision, hearing loss, malnutrition, family problems, poverty, and cultural deprivation—it is thought that developmental reading disorder or dyslexia affects fifteen percent of American school children (*Facts About Dyslexia* 1993). At present there is no universally agreed upon definition of dyslexia, but it can be considered a disorder in processing written language, i.e., reading and writing, with deficits in one or more of the following:

letter-sound associations,

decoding unknown words,

word recognition,

spelling (reversals, transpositions, insertions, omissions),

short-term memory,

name retrieval ability,

expressive writing,

reading comprehension,

speech, and

handwriting (Clark 1988).

To recognize adolescents with these problems in the classroom, however, is not always easy because each student is different and has a particular cluster of language deficits. The following brief profiles illustrate the variety of students a teacher might encounter.

Andy is articulate and intelligent, has a rich vocabulary, frequently asks and answers questions in class, and would like to go to college. When he is given a written assignment, however, he does not begin immediately, and may take most of the period "thinking about it." The paper he may complete, finally, will not contain the complex sentences or words he uses in his speech, but rather simple words and sentences because he fears making spelling errors.

Sarah is quiet and attentive. When given a written assignment, she writes slowly, compressing illegible words and sentence fragments into the center of her paper, ignoring the margins. She does not know how to compose a coherent paragraph or essay. When asked to rewrite her paper, she frequently has her mother type it for her. She is reluctant to discuss her reading and writing problems, and seldom asks for assistance.

James' I.Q score reveals average intelligence, but he has low self-esteem, and is reading three levels below his grade level. He has difficulty decoding words that have three or more syllables, and he writes illegibly to hide his spelling confusions. He often becomes angry, impatient, and frustrated with his academic tasks. He has little support from his family and does not want his peers to know he is labeled "learning disabled." Frequently in trouble with the authorities both in and out of school, he writes about dropping out of school, joining a gang, and selling drugs.

Amy works hard, has average intelligence, is good-natured and motivated, but is often the only girl in a class of slow readers. One of her teachers thinks she is "retarded." She does not understand many sound-symbol associations and tests poorly because by the time she finishes laboriously decoding words, she has forgotten the meaning of what she has read. Often, in her speech, she confuses words such as "fought" for "thought." She has strong family support for her problem, however, and frequently asks for help from her teachers.

Isaac behaves like a much younger child. He would rather joke with his friends than focus on his work. He is small for his age, impulsive, hyperactive, and has difficulty following directions. But when he listens to what is being presented in class, he understands and answers questions correctly. If quizzed orally, he remembers what he has learned, but if he responds in writing, his answers are often incomplete and ambiguous. He has trouble composing a well-organized paragraph, and he has problems with spelling and grammar. He, like Amy, has difficulty understanding the meaning of what he has read because of his word-by-word reading. When he does complete his assignments, he often misplaces or loses them. However, he makes good grades in math.

Jeff is intelligent, motivated, and plans to go to college. He has been aware of his specific reading disability for years; his parents have always supported and encouraged him. He asks for help in understanding the meaning of literary passages and in organizing paragraphs and essays. He reads slowly, and, unfortunately, because he is not receiving all the assistance he needs, he is making Cs instead of As in his academic work.

Beth comes from a family with a history of language disabilities. She is bright, artistic, confident, and well read. Her expressive writing, while loosely organized, is full of creative and imaginative ideas. She is also a phonetic speller and is likely to write "telefon" for "telephone," and to make letter reversals such as "flet" for "felt." Beth does not believe she will ever learn to write and to spell with more ease and accuracy. She accepts grades that do not reflect her ability.

Unfortunately, as Alice Ansara noted, many teachers also believe that it is too late to salvage the language potential of students with dyslexia; and this attitude, coupled with the difficulty of knowing how to assess and teach such students, diverse and unique as they are, lowers the prospects for students' success. Moreover, at this time, there are increasing expectations that students be capable of abstract thought, of fluent reading, and of putting their thoughts into writing—expectations that students with dyslexia cannot meet without assistance (Ansara1972a).

The students, themselves, having developed low self-esteem from years of academic failure, often find themselves in conflict with parents and teachers as they struggle to cope with the turmoil of adolescence, pressure from peers, and a desire for independence. Therefore, in order to reclaim the language capacity of these students, teachers of adolescents with dyslexia need support from counselors, principals, teachers, and parents in resolving the maze of emotional and social problems.

Chapter 2

Evaluation:
What is the Problem?

The first step in reading therapy is identification. For this, a careful assessment is necessary to determine the nature and severity of the disability. If a student has not been tested for learning disabilities, a referral for screening is initiated. This screening process includes an evaluation of visual and hearing acuity, a medical examination, a family history, and psychological and educational testing.

After medical problems have been ruled out, psychological and educational tests can provide useful data about students' reading difficulties. Alice Ansara advised that certain formal tests, however, give only general information, not the specific information one discovers in a diagnostic teaching session. Scores should not be regarded as definitive because students with long-time reading problems, who struggle with the decoding of words, often fail to grasp the significance of what they are reading. How students respond to test-taking is another relevant factor. After years of failure, many students with reading disabilities impulsively guess at answers or give up trying to answer correctly.

Ansara also believed that reading grade scores derived from standardized tests should not induce teachers to select high-interest, low vocabulary reading material. An adolescent with dyslexia needs to absorb the vocabulary of books with a rich language and high literary content. In addition, developmental levels should always be considered because many adolescents are capable of understanding more abstract patterns of thought. If taught to use cognitive skills and knowledge already acquired, an adolescent can make faster progress than a young child. Thus, the results of formal testing will give the teacher some idea of a student's reading deficits, but must be viewed judiciously (Ansara 1972a).

Informal assessments may yield more precise data about a student's performance.

Observations of students in the classroom indicate how attentive and motivated they are, and if they have developed behaviors that interfere with learning. If a student's behavior is troubling, a teacher should examine school records and/or obtain more information from other professionals who know the student.

Interviews with students also reveal much about their attitudes concerning personal goals, school, teachers, and learning.

A silent reading test gives a comparative score, but not specific information.

An oral reading test could indicate difficulties in sound-symbol associations, syllabication, phrasing, and comprehension. It is important to remember that words read in context produce different results from those read in isolation.

A paragraph completion test, untimed, can demonstrate how well students organize and express ideas in written language.

A dictated spelling test reveals what students know of spelling rules, and whether or not there are confusions such as substitutions, reversals, omissions, insertions, or transpositions. If students have difficulty with these in spelling, they will surely have trouble with them in silent reading. A list of nonsense syllables and words read aloud shows precisely what particular sounds, blends, or syllables students may not know.

A writing sample indicates problems in composition, development, sentence formation, thinking patterns, and spelling (*Classnotes* 1977).

DIAGNOSTIC READING SESSION

A diagnostic reading session is one of the most important means of gaining information about a student's reading problem. Sitting across from or at an angle to the student and following along with a copy of the book from which the student reads aloud, enables you, the teacher, to note guessing, hesitation, letter or word reversal, omission, insertion, vowel or consonant confusion, difficulty with digraph or diphthong, problems syllabicating words with one or more syllables, and lack of fluency. The diagnostic check sheet (see page 8), if used discreetly, may be of help in recording specific deficits.

MATURATIONAL DIFFERENCES

In addition to discovering what a student knows or does not know, be aware also of those students who have been called "immature" or "developmentally delayed." Among students labeled "learning disabled" in junior or senior high school, a high percentage, particularly boys, appear to be physically, emotionally, and/or cognitively immature. Current research supports the notion of gender bias in teacher referrals (Anderson 1997). However, many teachers wonder if the numbers of these developmentally delayed students with reading problems would decrease if reading readiness, rather than chronological age, were the determining factor for grade placement in the primary years.

In *Maturational Readiness for School Tasks* (1969), Ansara described educators, who, perceiving reading problems in the first and second grades, assume that students who are far behind their peers will, like desert plants, after a "rare sudden shower of rain . . . spontaneously burst into bloom"(p. 51). Unfortunately, as Ansara noted, regardless of whether the delay is caused by cultural deprivation, premature birth, or deviations in the nervous system, this blooming rarely occurs, and the student becomes an adolescent scarred by academic failure.

If you are a teacher of secondary students with reading difficulties, it is necessary to find out if students are capable of abstract thought or if they need manipulatives or graphic presentations to understand a concept. A sixteen-year-old, who is emotionally and cognitively twelve or thirteen years old, cannot be expected to match the performance or the behavior of a more mature student. If, for example, a student is having a problem understanding how to "narrow" a topic, it may be necessary to put a general topic, for instance "non-violence," on a large piece of cardboard. The more narrowed topic, "Martin Luther King," can be placed on a smaller piece of cardboard, and then the more limited topic, "The March on Selma," on an even smaller piece. There are many ways to present concepts to students, but first you must be able to identify their maturational levels. The student described above still needs graphic, "hands-on" demonstrations of ideas.

Finally, the results of formal and informal assessments will be an inventory of a student's strengths and weaknesses. You, as the teacher should discuss these results, including any misread items, with the student. As Ansara (1972b) pointed out, it is in the frank assessment of assets and liabilities, in the discussion of how reading disabilities develop, in the planning for remediation, and in the setting of goals that the necessary partnership between teacher and student is formed.

Diagnostic Check Sheet for Oral Reading Sessions

Student:

Errors	Monday	Tuesday	Wednesday	Thursday	Friday
consonants					
vowels					
blends (bl, br, cl, cr, fl, fr, gl, gr, pl, sl, sm, st, tr, -ft, -st, etc.)					
consonant digraphs (sh, ch, th, ph, wh)					
vce words					
vowel digraphs (ay, ai, ee, ea, ie, ei, oa, oe, aw, ou, ow, ue)					
syllable division					
reversals					
omissions					
substitutions					
insertions					
behavior: attitude guessing					
other					

SUGGESTIONS FOR NEW TEACHERS

Objective: Be prepared.

A. Before students arrive, determine how and when they will currently be evaluated in order that you can discuss strengths, deficits, and goals with each of them. Samples of written language can be obtained in group assessment.

B. Consult with regular teachers to learn more about your students, and arrange to have teachers send you weekly lesson plans. Do not rely on students to give you this information.

C. Establish a system of grading that includes systematic notebook checks and bringing necessary material to class. (Ascertain whether students are able to obtain necessary materials).

D. Remember that highly structured lesson plans with a variety of activities are more likely to keep your class in order than verbal monitoring.

E. Determine what consistent activities (or variations of the same) you will use to begin and end your class. For example, you may begin each day with an oral or written review of the previous day's lesson, and end by having students write at least five sentences (about what they have learned or what concerns they have) in the "Creative Writing" section of their notebooks. Students truly enjoy reading the remarks (about content, not misspellings) that teachers write in response.

F. Post rules for classroom behavior and discuss these with the students.

G. Keep your classroom attractive but uncluttered, and, on the walls, keep essays or creative writing and drawings by students to give them a sense of pride and "ownership."

H. Be sure you have an overhead projector or computer with screen in your classroom.

I. Ask the librarian if you can keep an old set of ency-clopedias in your room. Also have one set of dictio-naries, and class sets of books (perhaps those read in English class) novels, nonfiction, and plays. (Students enjoy the interrelatedness of playreading.)

J. Establish a place in your classroom for student notebooks. Keep extra three-ring binders for students who cannot afford to buy them.

K. Make copies of nonsense words and words for syl-labication and dictation and file in order of difficulty.

L. Keep two large three-ring binders for yourself. In one, file the initial written work of each student in order to compare it with writing completed at the end of the year. In the other, keep your daily lesson plans for absent students and your own evaluators.

M. Compose a paper for students and parents listing course objectives, explaining techniques and proce-dures necessary to improve reading, including a list of materials—paper, pens, three-ring binders—for students to take home and return signed by parents.

N. Finally, contact the parent(s) of each student not later than three weeks after school begins. It is of vital importance to keep in communication with parents, many of whom can be very supportive.

Chapter 3

Teaching: Principles and Strategies

Once the language problem has been targeted, you, as the teacher, may need the help of guidance counselors, administrators, and other teachers, to change negative behaviors of students who have experienced years of reading failure and have given up on teachers, school, and themselves. These adolescents need to be convinced that if they are able to develop the appropriate skills and language training, they can be successful. There is much to be accomplished and little time to lose. A first step is to designate a time and place for daily language remediation.

BASIC PRINCIPLES OF TEACHING

Alice Ansara believed that all students are unique and able to be taught if their individual modes of learning are understood and utilized. The following are some teaching principles that she considered applicable to all students.

1. Begin, not with a program, but by building on the knowledge, vocabulary, and concepts that students already possess.

2. Use students' most dominant learning modality—visual, auditory, kinesthetic, or tactile—and connect other modalities to it.

3. Avoid uncertainty in a learning sequence by presenting contrast rather than similarity.

4. Make certain students are confident and secure in what they have learned, particularly in the initial phase of each new task.

5. Analyze the segments of each learning task and establish a logical order of presentation.

6. Reassess students' understanding and readiness for each new learning task.

7. Use an approach that allows students to discover for themselves the sequence and meaning of each component in a learning task.

8. Review frequently to ensure that students retain what they have learned.

9. Proceed as rapidly from task to task as students' modes of learning and rates of assimilation permit.

10. Establish goals and objectives with students, and evaluate frequently their mastery and progress.

For adolescents with reading difficulties, Ansara urged teachers to explain that therapy takes time, that sometimes it is boring, and that an ideal for students to reach is reading two grade levels above their present grade. In addition, teachers can encourage students by showing them long and difficult words and assuring them that eventually they will be able to read such words (*Classnotes* 1977).

THE TWO-LEVEL APPROACH

Burdened with helping students keep up with their class-work and homework, you might be tempted to abandon the task of remediation or, determined to address language problems, give priority to this and ignore class requirements. Unfortunately, neither of these approaches, by itself, will save a student with dyslexia from academic failure.

Alice Ansara believed that because there is so little time, teachers of adolescents with specific language problems must work on two levels at the same time. One level encompasses teaching that will enable students to meet the requirements of their academic classes. The other level includes language training to help students overcome deficits in sound and symbol associations, syllabication, and/or vocabulary. Teaching on either of these levels involves reading, writing, spelling, and study skills (1972b).

Soon after school begins, you can assist students enormously by going through their texts and helping them become familiar with the formats. Teach them how to use the table of contents, index, and glossary, and how to anticipate the content of each chapter by reading the questions and summary at the end of each chapter. Have them note graphs, pictures, subtopics in bold print, and other clues to meaning (Ansara 1972b). While perusing textbooks with students, be aware if they are having difficulty reading words such as *glossary* and *appendix*. Begin language therapy by introducing these vocabulary words using a multisensory approach, so that in one period, working on both levels, you can prepare students for classroom instruction and for reading words that once seemed formidable.

A MULTISENSORY APPROACH

When teaching any adolescent, dyslexic student or not, be aware of how that student learns. Is the dominant learning modality visual, auditory, kinesthetic, or tactile? This information can be derived from observation and from testing. However, given time constraints for testing, overcrowded classrooms, and limited opportunities for teaching in small groups or one-on-one, it is important to create lesson plans with as many multisensory activities as possible to ensure that most students understand and learn.

Multisensory techniques have been used since the 1920s, when Grace Fernald developed her visual, auditory, kinesthetic, tactile (VAKT) approach in which students repeat aloud the names of words they are tracing (Clark 1988). Samuel Orton, a neurologist and psychiatrist, studied children with reading problems, and, based on his research, his colleague, Anna Gillingham, with Bessie Stillman, developed the Gillingham and Stillman (1956) manual for teaching children with dyslexia using multisensory techniques. One of these techniques, Simultaneous Oral Spelling (S.O.S), is used to reinforce both spelling and reading. In this procedure, a teacher pronounces a word, for example, *flat*, and names the letters. Students repeat the word *flat*, name the letters *f-l-a-t*, write each letter, naming the letter as they write it, *f-l-a-t*, and then repeat the word *flat*. Students are given auditory input from the sound of the teacher's voice and their own voices repeating what has been heard. Visual stimulus is given by seeing the letters, a kinesthetic stimulus as their hands form letters, and a visual-auditory-kinesthetic association as they name the letters, see them, and write them. Words are introduced in a carefully sequenced order, beginning with phonetic words and then later with nonphonetic words. Naming the letters rather than sounding them out helps students when nonphonetic words such as *cough* are introduced (Gillingham and Stillman 1956).

Although the principles of remediation in the Orton-Gillingham approach are the same for both younger and older students, the application of these procedures is different with older students. Elaborating on this point, Alice Ansara noted that older students, unless they cannot read at all, present problems such as slow reading, difficulty with expressive writing, poor comprehension and spelling, and a lack of study skills. Even though some of these problems can be addressed broadly, for example, by introducing vocabulary with dictionary skills, language training must be carefully structured to ensure that adolescents with dyslexia develop accuracy and fluency for decoding and writing.

Always tailor remediation to individual needs, keeping in mind that each student has a unique starting point, a varying accumulation of knowledge, and an individual set of problems (Ansara 1980). When asking students to record homework assignments, be sensitive to different learning styles. Write assignments legibly on the blackboard, read them aloud, give students time to record them and ask questions, and then check to see that most students have recorded them accurately. When giving students new science vocabulary words, write the words on the blackboard, pronounce them, have students repeat the words, and then have students write them in their notebooks. When beginning the study of a new country in geography, display a large topographical map labeled with cities, mountains, and plains for students to see and touch. All of these strategies represent modified multisensory teaching activities that increase the learning potential of most students.

For a student with more severe reading problems, a homework assignment may be recorded inaccurately because the student writes slowly and reverses page numbers. A list of vocabulary words, copied from the blackboard, may be incomplete because of slow handwriting and deciphering written symbols incorrectly. Before geography class, a student may take so much time trying to find the right book in a disorganized locker that he or she comes to class late, does not notice the topographical map, feels frustrated, embarrassed, and inclined either to withdraw or to be disruptive. For this student, provide, on a daily basis, a structured, safe, and positive environment where such academic mishaps can be alleviated and self-confidence restored. Help the student organize his or her locker, survey the chapter about the new country in the geography text, including maps, graphs, subtopics, and questions. Allow him or her enough time to copy the math homework assignment. If necessary, copy the vocabulary list from a science text and give it to the student. When introducing new vocabulary, break each word into syllables, naming the syllables and having the student repeat them, while looping under each syllable with a pencil.

Have the student write the word and say it again.

phos ˌpho ˌres ˌcence

Using a pencil for syllabication is a highly effective multi-sensory technique. For students with more persistent reading difficulties, writing words in bold letters on the blackboard, pronouncing the words, and naming the letters while tracing over them with chalk, may also help. When explaining to students how multisensory techniques enhance memory, you might cite the example of someone, who, having made a list of items to be purchased, forgets the list, but remembers the items, simply because of the kinesthetic act of having written them down.

THE PENCILING TECHNIQUE

A common sight in a resource room or regular classroom is that of students with slow reading skills laboriously reading aloud and trying to help themselves by using their fingers to focus on individual words. Often such students have a history of being corrected by elementary teachers for this practice, so that, as adolescents, they continue to use fingers for focus but do so with embarrassment and shame, even under the aegis of more knowing teachers. One of Alice Ansara's most successful techniques for students with dyslexia is that of penciling. She developed this procedure after reading Dr. Orton's account of his use of pencil facilitation with stutterers (1937). Ansara believed that using a pencil for focus, coordinating eye and brain, helps students eliminate reversals, transpositions, insertions and omissions, and other inaccuracies. She also believed that penciling helps students recognize syllables and affixes, identify key words and phrases, and improve reading comprehension.

The five sequential stages of penciling

For students with severe reading problems, who frequently omit words and have difficulty reading the first letter or sound in a word, tracing the initial letter of each word enhances word awareness.

After the battle, the emperor, Asoka, walked among the dead and dying warriors, and he was filled with sorrow and repentance. This was a crucial turning point in his life, and he vowed never to undertake a military campaign again.

After a few weeks, if these students are reading with more precision, they can more easily mark under the first letter of each word.

After the battle, the emperor, Asoka, walked among the dead and dying warriors, and he was filled with sorrow and repentance. This was a crucial turning point in his life, and he vowed never to undertake a military campaign again.

Discontinue this stage of penciling as soon as a student is able to read accurately and is ready to begin phrasing. Swinging the pencil beneath phrases will increase fluency and comprehension. Students who do not recognize signal words—words that anticipate meaning such as *but, although, since, before, after*— can circle these while phrasing.

After the battle, the emperor, Asoka, walked among the dead and dying warriors, and he was filled with sorrow and repentance. This was a crucial turning point in his life, and he vowed never to undertake a military campaign again.

After phrasing has been mastered, students will be reading with more speed, and will simply underline sentences.

After the battle, the emperor, Asoka, walked among the dead and dying warriors, and he was filled with sorrow and repentance. This was a crucial turning point in his life, and he vowed never to undertake a military campaign again.

Eventually, they can begin to syllabicate words and circle special elements such as affixes, isolated for recognition, until they become fluent readers.

After the battle, the emperor, Asoka, walked among the dead and dying warriors, and he was filled with sorrow and repentance. This was a crucial turning point in his life, and he vowed never to undertake a military campaign again.

Remember that each student begins penciling at a different stage depending on his or her disability, and continues working at that stage for only as long as it is necessary (Ansara 1972b; 1977).

Ansara used the following quotation from John Steinbeck's *The Red Pony* to illustrate how a student would use penciling for syllabication, isolating phrases, and circling plurals, affixes, and vowel digraphs (overhead).

Sometimes if the work horses were to be used that day, Jody found Billy Buck in the barn, harnessing and currying. Billy stood with him and looked at Gabilan and he told Jody a great many things about horses. He explained that they were terribly afraid for their own feet, so that one must make a practice of lifting their legs and patting the hoofs and ankles to remove their terror. He told Jody how horses love conversation. He must talk to the pony all the time, and tell him the reasons for everything.

Make notes of any difficulties students may have with particular sounds or words for later review. While there is a need for it, the pencil must be used for all oral or silent reading. If students object to a practice they think more suited to elementary-aged children, convince them that consistent use of the penciling technique is crucial for success in reading.

THE STUDENT NOTEBOOK

Disorganization is a common characteristic of many students with specific language disabilities. Often, I am sure, you have watched students search frantically through backpacks or notebooks for missing homework, or present for inspection notebooks covered with drawings, doodles, and names, containing incomplete sets of papers, some of which have been torn out and refiled in great disarray. This disorganization bodes ill for students, as this inattention and messiness usually carries over into college or job. When discussing goals with students, be sure they understand that all their work has value and, therefore, should be carefully organized in their notebooks. Explain that keeping papers in sequential order is an essential time-saving skill that will be used later in life when filing important papers, bills, receipts for taxes, or other information.

Alice Ansara believed that the primary work of language training is reflected in the student notebook. As a learning tool, the notebook becomes a source of pride and security because it will always be there as a reference and reminder of what the student has accomplished (*Classnotes* 1977). According to Ansara, the student notebook is a vital part of remediation. It is used for syllabication, vocabulary, spelling, phrasing and signal words, sentences and paragraphs, essays, study skills, and creative writing, all carefully labeled and in special sections. The notebook should be a three-ring binder, neatly organized, and kept in the classroom at all times. For academic survival, it is more important that students be able to read than to spell; therefore, the first objective is accurate and fluent reading. Give students passages and lists of words to decode and to read aloud on a daily basis. Because students use pencils for decoding and the S.O.S. approach for dictation, spelling improvement should inevitably occur.

Carefully explain the procedure for words read from lists and words written from dictation, both filed in the student notebook.

1. Choose a list of polysyllabic words for students who have problems with syllabication. Ask students to read the words, while using pencils to divide them into syllables.

2. After students read an entire page correctly, fold the page and date it.

3. One week later, review the words, and if the students pronounce one or more incorrectly, reopen the page and have the students start again.

4. Two weeks later, review this same page, and, if all the words are read correctly, have the students fold their pages permanently, date them, and file them in their notebooks under the category of "syllabication." If a student, for various reasons, continues to have problems reading or spelling particular words, include these words in later lists rather than have the student repeat the same list many times.

Student Notebook	
	categories
The notebook will contain: 1) sounds and nonsense words, words with two or more syllables, vocabulary, phrases and sentences given to a student for reading, and lists of dictated words for spelling; 2) exercises for study skills, spelling rules, and inductive thinking; 3) models of sentences, paragraphs, and essays, used for study and reference; and 4) sentences, paragraphs, essays, poems, and stories written by the students.	**sounds and symbols**
	syllable division
	vocabulary
	spelling
	phrases and signal words
	Sentences and paragraphs
	essays
	study skills
	creative writing

Student Notebook	
	categories
This category will contain lists of words for reading and dictation: 1) closed syllable (<u>bus</u>); 2) vowel consonant-E syllables (<u>lake</u>); 3) open syllables (<u>go</u>); 4) R-controlled syllables (<u>bird</u>); 5) vowel digraph and diphthong syllables (<u>boat</u>, <u>cow</u>); and 6) consonant-LE-syllables (<u>bundle</u>). **It will also contain definitions for words such as:** 1) syllable, 2) blend, 3) digraph, 4) diphthong. (To form tab for each section, cut out shaded area.)	**sounds and symbols** **cut out shaded area**

Student Notebook	
	categories
This category will include words for reading and dictation that represent the three rules of syllable division.	
1) Division between two consonants preceded and followed by single vowels	**syllable division**
2) Division after an open vowel and before a single consonant	
3) Division between two vowels that do not make one sound	
Words such as nouns, verbs, and adjectives will also be included.	

Student Notebook	
	categories
This category will include Latin, Greek, and Anglo-Saxon roots and affixes for reading, study, and dictation.	
It will also include definitions of terms such as *root*, *prefix*, *suffix*, and *assimilation*.	
	vocabulary

Student Notebook	
	categories

This category in the notebook includes four subdivisions:
1) Special Categories
 	
    a. words from class assignments
 	
    b. word patterns
 	
    c. vowel digraphs and homonyms
 	
2) Nonphonetic words
 	
3) Spelling Rules and Generalizations
 	
4) Dictation	

	spelling

	categories
Student Notebook	
This category will contain: 1) definitions of terms such as *phrase, signal word,* and *sentence;* 2) exercises in the use of phrasing and signal words; 3) models illustrating phrasing and signal words; 4) sentence-combining exercises; and 5) phrases for reading and dictation.	
	phrases and signal words

Student Notebook	
	categories
This category will include: 1) kinds of sentences; 2) models of paragraphs to be studied for main ideas, and facts and examples supporting the main idea; and 3) sentences and paragraphs written by the student.	
	sentences and paragraphs

Student Notebook	
	categories

This category will contain:

1) models of essays to be read and studied;

2) exercises in narrowing a topic and writing a main idea;

3) more discussion and examples on how to support the main idea and to provide transitions between paragraphs; and

4) essays that state an opinion, compare and contrast, and descriptive essays, written by students.

essays

Student Notebook	
	categories

This category will include any exercises concerned with these study skills.

1) surveying a textbook

2) learning how to study

3) notetaking

4) making an outline

5) studying for tests

6) using a dictionary

7) using the library

8) writing a research paper

study skills

	categories
Student Notebook	
This category may contain journals, stories, and poems written for particular classes or simply for self-expression.	
If the writing is for a class assignment, students will probably need assistance in editing and rewriting. If students want a teacher merely to read a story or poem, he or she should read it, give positive feedback, and refrain from editing the writing unless asked to do so. Misspellings or poor sentence structure may be noted, but discussed at another time.	
The adolescent with dyslexia may also be an unusually gifted writer. In this case, the teacher should not only encourage this strength, but try to make other teachers aware of the student's writing ability. In addition, if any students are talented artists, they should be encouraged to keep drawings in this section.	
	creative writing

Closed Syllables, Short Vowels					ă
VC	CVC	CCVC	CVCC	CCVCC	
at	saf	frat	sand	frast	
ab	sap	drat	rast	plaft	
an	tam	spat	dast	plast	
am	fam	plat	nast	brasp	
as	lax	tram	baft	tramp	
ad	ras	plam	past	clamp	
ax	qat	slat	sast	flast	
av	sas	pram	mast	blant	
al	maf	blan	tasp		
ap	jad	fran	ramp		
	pas	snaf			
	wat	praf			
	wam	frax			
	cam				
	dat				

Example of Notebook Page in Section on Sounds and Symbols.

Closed Syllables, Short Vowels					DIGRAPHS
VC	CVC	CCVC	CVCC	CCVCC	
aph	chat	throm	marph	chrond	
esh	biph	thraf	sumph	frosht	
oth	posh	pluth	blith	sterph	
ush	tach	drick	chust	phlost	
ith	quth	gleph	pholt	chlept	
ach	whish	brock	thant	shlond	
eph	wuth	prith	whist	gresht	
ish	wuth	thrub	shemp	drasht	
och	reth	phlet	chast	blunch	
uph	phum	groph	whuft	phrond	
ack	naph	thrut	chilt	chlisp	
ech	bock	glaph	lepht	chling	
ick	jiph	blick	sholb	phrunt	
oph	wush	plesh	thilk	glanch	
uth	kish	druph	phent	shlipt	
ash	chim	bruch	chulb	fronch	
eck	poth	flaph	shink	flinch	
ich	whum	closh	wholt	blanch	
ock	taph	blith	thost	trunch	
uch	gesh	steph	whent	chrest	

Example of Notebook Page in Section on Sounds and Symbols.

CVC	⌒ VCV	CVC	⌒ VCV
hop	hope	fuss	fuse
rob	robe	tack	stake
cut	cute	lock	bloke
rip	ripe	pock	poke
fat	fate	doll	dole
us	use	bill	bile
tap	tape	pill	pile
can	cane	chaff	chafe
tub	tube	duck	duke
mop	mope	back	bake
rip	tripe		
tin	tine		
pin	spine		
pal	pale		
win	twine		
rat	rate		
not	note		
trip	stripe		
cub	cube		
kit	kite		
win	wine		
not	note		
gap	gape		
rip	gripe		

(From an Ansara Overhead)

Example of Notebook Page in Section on Sounds and Symbols.

tion			-tion
/_shun_/			
na		tion	nation
mo		tion	motion
lo		tion	lotion
sta		tion	station
men		tion	mention
con	ven	tion	convention
com	mo	tion	commotion
re	la	tion	relation
sen	sa	tion	sensation
do	na	tion	donation
in	fla	tion	inflation
in	jec	tion	injection
se	lec	tion	selection
con	nec	tion	connection
re	jec	tion	rejection
pro	jec	tion	projection
va	ca	tion	vacation
for	ma	tion	formation
per	fec	tion	perfection
cor	rec	tion	correction
cor	rup	tion	corruption

Example of Notebook Page in Section on Syllable Division.

Closed Syllables, Short Vowels					Syllable Division I VCCV
dul	cet			*dulcet*	
pen	cil			*pencil*	
wan	ton			*wanton*	
at	ten	tion		*attention*	
con	ven	tion		*convention*	
con	nec	tion		*connection*	
thun	der	bolt		*thunderbolt*	
hob	gob	lin		*hobgoblin*	
com	pul	sion		*compulsion*	
gin	ger	bread		*gingerbread*	
es	tab	lish		*establish*	
part	ner	ship		*partnership*	
in	trin	sic		*intrinsic*	
cen	sor	ship		*censorship*	
at	ten	tion		*attention*	
in	ter	cep	tion	*interception*	
in	con	des	cent	*incondescent*	
un	sus	pec	ting	*unsuspecting*	
dis	con	nec	tion	*disconnection*	
in	ter	as	tive	*interactive*	
in	sub	stan	tial	*insubstantial*	
im	per	cep	tive	*imperceptive*	

Example of Notebook Page in Section on Syllable Division.

Vowel Consonant Vowel					Syllable Division II
to	day				VCV
du	plex				
fro	zen				
mi	nor				
ty	rant				
to	ken				
ha	ven				
pro	pane				
Ja	son				
gro	cer				
si	mu	late			
mi	cro	scope			
mi	gra	tion			
ju	bi	lee			
re	la	tive			
mu	ta	tion			
se	di	tion			
e	ro	sion			
e	va	po	rate		
du	pli	ci	ty		
hy	po	der	mic		
hy	po	the	sis		

Right column words: today, duplex, frozen, minor, tyrant, token, haven, propane, Jason, grocer, simulate, microscope, migration, jubilee, relative, mutation, sedition, erosion, evaporate, duplicity, hypodermic, hypothesis

C U T

Example of Notebook Page in Section on Syllable Division.

Two Vowels, Two Sounds					Syllable Division III
sci	ence				*science*
cli	ent				*client*
qui	et				*quiet*
gi	ant				*giant*
ru	in				*ruin*
ki	osk				*kiosk*
tri	ad				*triad*
nu	cle	us			*nucleus*
he	ro	ic			*heroic*
nau	se	a			*nausea*
a	li	en			*alien*
di	a	ry			*diary*
si	es	ta			*siesta*
ka	o	lin			*kaolin*
hi	a	tus			*hiatus*
Ro	me	o			*Romeo*
li	a	ble			*liable*
o	a	sis			*oasis*
ba	o	bab			*baobab*
sco	li	o	sis		*scoliosis*
va	ri	e	ty		*variety*
o	be	di	ent		*obedient*

(Syllable Division column: V/V)

Example of Notebook Page in Section on Syllable Division.

Vowel consonant E and doubling rules

word	suffix	word anslysis	problem	solution	new word
hop	-ing	VC + V	protect. sh. v	double c	hopping
hope	-ing	VCE + V	2 vowels	drop e	hoping
hope	-ful	VCE + C	O.K.	add suffix	hopeful
hope	-less	VCE + C	O.K.	add suffix	hopeless
back	-ing	VCC + V	O.K.	add suffix	backing
bake	-ing	VCE + V	2 vowels	drop e	baking
bank	-ing	VCC + V	O.K.	add suffix	banking
bark	-ing	VCC + V	O.K.	add suffix	barking
like	-ness	VCE + C	O.K.	add suffix	likeness
like	-ly	VCE + C	O,K,	add suffix	likely
slope	-ed	VCE + E	2 vowels	drop e	sloped
slop	ed	VC + V	protect sh. v	double c	slopped
slop	-y	VC + V	protect sh. v	double c	sloppy

(From an Ansara Overhead)

spelling

CUT

Example of Notebook Page in Section on Spelling.

Time: First Two Weeks
(always adjusted according to need)

PLANNING SUGGESTIONS

I. Objectives: Students will understand the two-level approach, the importance of constructing a language notebook, and techniques such as Simultaneous Oral Spelling (S.O.S.) and penciling. They will also understand how to survey their textbooks.

II. Materials: For notebook construction: Three-ring binders, paper, pens, pencils, rulers
For surveying textbooks: Student texts
For Simultaneous Oral Spelling: Lists of words from course texts and commonly misspelled words
For penciling: Paragraphs, magazines, texts in which students can underline

III. Procedures:

A. Explain that for academic success, students will work each day on two levels: learning the skills that will help them keep up with their course work and remediate their individual language deficits. For this work, they will learn how to survey their textbooks, construct notebooks, and use techniques such as S.O.S. and penciling. Also explain that *fifteen to twenty minutes of each period will be spent reading aloud (always using a pencil)* and *ten to fifteen minutes will be used for dictation using the S.O.S. technique.* Then, when students are prepared, have them construct a notebook, learn how to survey texts, and to use the S.O.S. and penciling techniques.

B. Before students begin constructing their notebooks, check to be certain all students have a three-ring binder, pens, and paper. Then give each student a ruler and scissors, and direct them to make tabs on different pages labeled in descending order—*sounds and symbols, syllable division, vocabulary, spelling, phrasing and signal words, sentences and paragraphs, essays, study skills, and creative writing*—and to cut out an inch-and-a-half strip of paper beneath the tabs. The notebooks will remain in the classroom at all times.

C. Direct students to bring their science, history, and math books to class at various times to survey texts. You may ask students to preview a text before they come to class. Then you can question them about the meanings of the words *glossary, index, preface, table of contents,* or *bibliography.* The words can be divided into syllables on the blackboard, and pronounced by teacher and students. After a cursory inspection of a text, chapter study begins. Students are taught to begin with the introduction (perhaps reading this aloud), then after glancing at the headings in bold print, at the graphs and pictures, and words in bold print or italics, to proceed to the questions and summary at the end. You may reverse this process in another chapter, starting at the end and then going back to the beginning. After this discussion, students are given exercises in which certain information is found in the book or in a particular chapter.

D. Before introducing the penciling technique, you will already have evaluated the students, and you will know if there are any students with severe reading problems, who may need to begin oral reading by tracing the first letter of each word. Most will begin by underlining the first letter of each word. Explain that as soon as they begin to read more fluently and more accurately, students will begin looping the pencil under phrases and later drawing a line under sentences. Students individually or in small groups will be reading from the same paragraphs or texts, on which, ideally, they can make marks. Record reading difficulties on the Diagnostic Check Sheet.

E. Using the blackboard or overhead, introduce the S.O.S. technique by showing the students a word and naming it, then having students say the word, write it, naming the letters (if necessary), and saying the word again. Dictate ten words (from texts, lists of commonly misspelled words, or words misspelled by your students) using the S.O.S. technique. If the words are spelled correctly, have students file them in their notebook under the spelling section. For reinforcement, students can also use the words in sentences or paragraphs.

IV. Evaluation: Have students make a list of the various strategies they need to use in order to improve their reading ability. Inspect their notebooks at consistent intervals. Give students information to find in the entire text and in one chapter of the text. Record the number and kinds of errors students make when reading aloud while using a pencil, and the accuracy of their spelling when using the S.O.S. technique.

Chapter 4

Sounds and Symbols

Having previously identified students' particular areas of need, you may find that many adolescents with dyslexia already know much about the basic sounds and symbols presented in this chapter. Students may, instead, have problems with syllabication, in which case that is exactly where teaching should begin. If, during a diagnostic teaching session, you note vowel or consonant confusions as students read aloud, focus on that particular problem before proceeding further. Some vowel confusions such as /ĭ/ and /ĕ/ are regional, and this should be discussed with students. Students with severe dyslexia, however, may be unable to discriminate short vowel sounds, especially in spelling. For these students, Alice Ansara advised a kinesthetic approach. By having students touch the tops of their throats, becoming aware of tongue and mouth positions when saying short words, *ed, ox, an, if, us,* and holding the vowel sounds a little longer, students may be able to detect differences in sound. After practicing this enough, they can make a chart of tongue positions for vowel sounds similar to the one below and put it in their notebooks:

at	a	
Ed	e	
it	i	
on	o	
up	u	

(Ansara, *Chart of Tongue Positions for Short Vowel Sounds,* 1972b)

Ansara also used a diagram for vowel production in English to illustrate how vowels are produced by the tongue in varying positions, high to low and front to back. A word like *up*, for example, is produced with the tongue in a mid-position for the low short *u* sound.

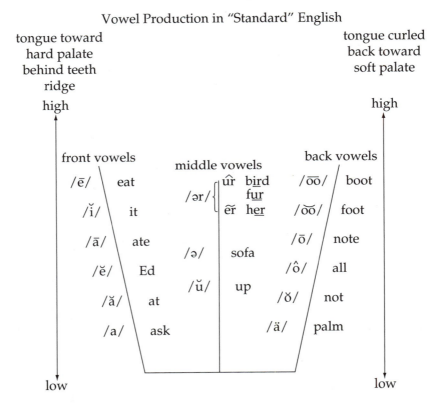

Diagram for Vowel Production in English from Ansara Overhead

Next, teach a syllable as a single unit of sound. (Do not simply give students the definition.) Students will also learn that there are six kinds of syllables:

1) Closed Syllables, which are formed when a single short vowel is enclosed by two consonants:

cat   top   cup   sip   wet

The vowel can also be enclosed by consonant digraphs (two letters with one sound):

that   shed   Mack   chat   whet

and by blends (consonants that slide together as they precede or follow a vowel):

graph   trash   flack   stick   blind

2) Vowel-Consonant-E Syllables (in which the positional e makes the first vowel long).

lake   mote   ride   Pete   duke

3) Open Syllables (in which the vowel is long because it is not blocked by a consonant):

go   flu   me   fly   ra

4) R-Controlled Syllables:

bird   fur   for   star   pert

5) Vowel Digraph and Diphthong Syllables (a vowel digraph represents two vowels that make one sound (pie) and a diphthong represents two vowels that blend into one another (cow):

pay   boat   pie   cow   loud

6) Consonant-LE Syllables:

bubble bundle bagle   truffle   sparkle   sample

Before beginning the exercises in this chapter, and for purposes of discussion and general knowledge, explain terms such as *vowel, consonant, blend, syllable, closed syllable, vowel-consonant-e syllable, open syllable, R-controlled syllable, vowel and consonant digraphs, trigraphs*, and *diphthongs*. According to Ansara, one of the reasons students do not learn is that they are often given definitions to memorize rather than examples and attributes that enable them to formulate their own definitions. Ansara thought that if reading were truly to become a reasoning process, it should begin at this basic level (Ansara 1977).

Therefore, when presenting the terms mentioned above, follow a modified version of the concept attainment model of Joyce, Weil, and Showers (1992). This model is based on a study of inductive thinking by Bruner (1977) in which students learn a concept by a process in which examples and nonexamples are presented. Students compare and contrast the examples of nouns, and other parts of speech until they are able to identify nouns by their characteristics or attributes. The model has three phases: phase one, in which data is presented to students; phase two, in which students categorize unlabeled data; and phase three, in which students analyze the method by which they arrived at conclusions. The third phase may be difficult for some students, so it is necessary to determine carefully the varying applications of the model.

1) FORMULATING A DEFINITION

Students already know that *a vowel is a speech sound in which air passes continuously through the open mouth* and that *a consonant is a speech sound made by obstructing the air stream.* Begin with the term, *digraph.* Make two headings on the blackboard: one labeled *digraphs* and one, *other.* Write two sets of words under the headings.

digraphs	other
phone	top
graph	cat

Ask students to look at the two sets of words and think about how they are alike and how they are different. Listen to the students' comments, and then put two more words under the headings, naming the words and having students name them:

that   pen

Ask students what characteristics *graph* and *that* have in common that *pen* and *cat* do not. Put two more words under the headings, pronouncing them as usual and asking students to pronounce them.

hush   hut

Ask students to write a definition of digraph. If students have severe writing problems, ask them to "think" about the definition. After the students finish writing, put more words under the headings.

chip	lip
ship	hip

After presenting six more pairs of words, ask students if they think the definitions they have formulated are correct. Write more words on the blackboard—*mush, man, top, sip, cup, rend*—and ask individual students to place them in one of the two categories.

Ask students under which heading *mush* should be placed. Proceed in this way, introducing words for students to categorize in the correct columns. When you are convinced that all students are able to correctly categorize digraphs and nondigraphs, ask students to share their definitions. If students understand that *a digraph is two letters that make one sound*, ask them to put their definitions in the appropriate section of their notebooks. Initially, this exercise may be difficult for students, but if they repeat it in learning other concepts, it will become easier and will enhance their ability to learn.

2) READING NONSENSE WORDS

The object of this exercise is to enable students to read one-syllable nonsense words with digraphs. Provide students with a list of words but keep a copy of the same list on which to note inaccuracies.

shab	whum	chim	thip	phen
bith	chet	toph	fath	dack
moph	luph	sheck	thim	whal
niph	wheck	shash	chub	hoth
gesh	photh	chuph	whiph	shan

After you read the list, have students read the list, either with you or alone, always with pencils in hand, underlining each word as it is pronounced. As was explained in Chapter 3, if a student reads the list with 100% accuracy, fold and date it, and have the student place it in his or her notebook, to be reviewed in one week. If the student does not read with 100% accuracy, reopen the page and repeat the exercise until the student is successful. In two weeks, review it again, then fold it permanently.

3) DICTATION

On a piece of lined notebook paper, have students draw four vertical lines about an inch-and a-half apart (see model notebook page on page 30) and mark "digraphs" as an identifying tab in the upper right corner. On the top of the page, have students write, *closed syllables, short vowels*. Beneath this, and consecutively above the five divisions, the students write *vc*, *cvc*, *ccvc*, *cvcc* and *ccvcc*. Begin dictation using the Simultaneous Oral Spelling technique.

1) Pronounce the nonsense word *aph* (digraphs are considered one consonant).

2) Have students say the word *aph* and spell it aloud, *a-p-h*

3) Have students write the word under the vc category, while saying the letters.

4) Have students say the word again, while underlining it with a pencil.

You may dictate more vc words, such as *ach*, *ath*, *ash*. Then, if students write these easily, dictate cvc words such as *thas*, *cham*, *phap*. Later, when you are certain the students have mastered these sounds, and, after blends have been introduced, proceed with ccvc words—*shrap*, *phlat*, *throm*; cvcc words—*rapht*, *balch*, *rasht*; and finally, with ccvcc words—*chlamp*, *phront*, *shlast*.

When reviewing blends, vowel digraphs, and other kinds of syllables, follow the same procedures for formulating definitions (if this is necessary), for reading, and for dictation.

With reference to teaching basic sounds and symbols, Alice Ansara gave this advice to teachers: 1) never teach sounds in isolation; 2) go from the simple to the complex; and 3) move as quickly as possible, but as slowly as necessary, in order to ensure success (Ansara 1977). Finally, convince students that these basic skills are essential if they want to become proficient readers.

/ĕ/ CLOSED SYLLABLES WITH SHORT VOWELS

Ted, trek, then, step, crest, bent, felt, pen, blend, mess

b e f	b l e p	b e f f	b r e n g
d e v	d r e f	d e l g	d r e m p
p e s	p r e d	p e s h	p l e n t
m e s	m e v	m e l k	m e f f
f e t	f r e s s	f e m p	f r e s k
n e p	n e t h	n e f t	n e b s
y e n	y e n t	y e l k	y e s t
l e d	l e s h	l e b t	l e m t
j e m	j e s p	j e l p	j e t h

cez	cred	celp	chent
sed	slep	shelt	spelt
zep	zet	zess	zeng
wef	whem	welp	whesk
ket	kem	kesp	kest
reb	rep	reft	retch
tes	tret	temp	trend
phep	phek	phest	phelk
thet	thed	then	themp

/ă/ CLOSED SYLLABLES WITH SHORT VOWELS

tap, nap, trap, cram, sham, chap, black, smack, flap, rap

ban	brand	blam	bask
crad	clad	cant	cash
dab	drat	dwat	dand
fram	fant	flask	frab
gant	glasp	grad	galp
hamp	hask	hack	hapt
jaft	jalp	jask	jant
kan	kant	krack	kras
lam	lasp	laft	lash
mand	mank	mask	match
natch	nath	nast	naph
pak	plask	pramp	patch
quap	quand	qual	quas
raft	ratch	rag	rasp
saf	shad	spand	slam
tam	talc	tasp	trank
vast	vash	vrasp	vald

w a m	w a s t	w h a m	w a k
y a k	y a p h	y a t c h	y a n d
z a x	z a f t	z a s k	z a p
t h a n	t h a p h	t h a x	t h a s
m a n s k	n a f t	s p a l	l a s k
f l a m	s p r a t	m a l f	r a s t
s h a l t	s h a f t	s h a m	s h a s k

/ĭ/ CLOSED SYLLABLES WITH SHORT VOWELS Y /ĭ/

sit, bit, split, trip, quick, dip, chick, fit, rip, clip, ship, nip

t i b	t r i b	t i s p	t r i n t
s i f	s l i f	s m i t c h	s p i n d
r i s	r i m p	r i n t	r i l b
d i s	d i c t	d r i c t	d i l f
f i p	f r i n k	f i m p	f l i f t
m i v	m i s k	m i l p	m i p h
b i x	b r i t	b l i n g	b i l b
p i l	p l i n	p r i s k	p i l d
j i t	j i f f	j i l p	j i s t
k i l	k i n t	k i t h	k r i n k
n i x	n i s p	n i t c h	n i m
l i z	l i c t	l i n d	l i s t
h i x	h i f t	h i m p	h i l l
q u i l	q u i n t	q u i l p	q u i s t
y i v	y i l f	y i s k	y i s p
w i f	w i s c	w h i z	w h i n t
v i n	z i s h	v i f t	z i n t
c r i n	g l i s t	g r i f t	k r i p
t r i p h	p h i x	c h i n d	s h r i m p

g r y p h	s y l l	f l y n t	r y f t
m y t h	s p r y n t	s m y t h	p y t h
l y n d	k y t h	b l y m p	d y s t
d r y p	p l y d	s p y f f	k r y p t

/ŏ/ CLOSED SYLLABLES WITH SHORT VOWELS

top, mop, slot, stop, crop, cot, rock, clock, bond, lost

b o p	b l o x	b o n g	b r o n
c o n	c l o k	c o n k	c r o f t
d o s	d r o g	d o l t	d r o n d
f o z	f r o t	f o n t	f l o t c h
g o n	g r o d	g o f t	g l o c t
h o b	h o t h	h o l p	h o s s
j o f	j o n g	j o p h	j o s h
k o v	k r o m	k o l t	k r o c k
l o j	l o f f	l o n t	l o n k
m o f t	m o d g e	m o s h	m o t c h
n o z	n o c t	n o m p	n o t h
p o g	p r o b	p o n t	p l o s s
q u o d	q u o f t	q u o d g e	q u o c k
r o x	r o n g	r o t h	r o l f
s o p	s w o g	s m o c k	s l o s t
t o v	t r o s k	t h o t	t r o m p
v o d	v o c h	v o n d	v r o m
w o f	y o f f	z o p h	w h o n d
d r o t	d o p	d o n d	d r o t h
g r o f t	g o s t	g l o t	g o m p
t r o m	t h o n	t r o p h	t o m s
k o s t	k r o s	k o p h	k o s h

bloth	broph	shob	chot
chol	cros	phroc	shock

/ŭ/ CLOSED SYLLABLES WITH SHORT VOWELS

cup, mud, cut, truck, dug, gum, up, hug, rug, chum

cum	crup	culp	clusp
buv	bruf	buft	blund
gup	glump	gump	grust
juc	junt	julp	juff
mus	mut	munk	mund
pud	prug	pund	plumt
rux	ruff	runt	rudge
duz	drut	dunt	drung
huv	hulb	hudge	hump
kul	krut	kudge	krutch
fuff	flus	fung	frunk
lut	luft	lud	lumt
nug	nuss	num	nut
sud	sluj	scuph	smunk
tun	tuth	trump	trush
vub	vrug	vulp	vrunch
wut	wutch	wuld	whusk
yuk	yulb	yud	yush
thus	thug	shunt	shush
phun	phump	plum	scrum
zun	zuft	zuck	zudge
shung	swung	shrun	slusk
chulp	cruf	chruph	shruph

OPEN VOWELS

shy, no, fry, my, go, hi, by, we, so, he, she, flu,

d a	r e	m o	d u
s l a	f i	s k o	t u
s h i	d r e	n u	g l y
b r a	s p e	d r o	s l u
p h a	f l o	s m i	d r u
t h y	s m e	b r o	f r u
s k a	b l e	s n o	t w y
r a	s e	b r i	s t u
t h a	g l e	s n y	b r i
f l a	z e	w h i	s l o
c h u	f e	s h o	d o
g r a	f r e	p l u	p h o
f a	v e	l u	q u i
c o	s h r i	q u e	t r u
c y	t h r e	s p o	t y
g y	n u	b l o	f r i
p h r u	t r e	s y	w u
z i	p h o	s n u	s p u
c r i	f l i	t h r o	s m a
r u	s m a	t u	q u o
d w i	f u	p r i	s t a
s k e	g l u	s n i	y i
b l u	s p h u	s q u a	p h r o

VOWEL - CONSONANT - e SYLLABLES

The second vowel in this syllable is silent, but it makes the preceding vowel long.

ace, hope, time, type, flute, Pete, wipe, same, mule, date, fine, home, kite,

pate	mise	jute	lene	mone
gane	dyte	lune	mete	rone
bate	lipe	mune	sele	zome
rale	cyfe	yuve	dene	doke
dule	beze	hone	bide	kage
fane	syme	lute	peve	cote
hape	cride	vune	meke	wole
wafe	dive	lume	zebe	strode
quate	tryne	thuse	grene	probe
abe	ide	krule	whete	phobe
afe	wives	pruce	thene	jove
trave	quine	yude	pheze	chode
stade	jibe	ute	wheme	thove
phame	type	shute	hepe	stome

R - CONTROLLED SYLLABLES

Bert, bird, fern dart, sport, mirth, Ford, dirt, yarn, part, art

ferm	wirth	surb	mord	nard
derf	clirm	turg	norp	starph
kers	hirth	churl	stort	sharn
gerb	jirx	shurm	yorm	parx
berg	quirk	burth	gorz	clarm
sterph	virst	wurst	horst	targ
sherl	hird	kurd	cort	charl
cert	blirb	clurm	nord	blark
blerp	girt	purth	morph	karp
flerv	hirsh	yurt	jorst	darf
clerk	virb	clurb	sorf	zart
yern	jir	sturf	clorm	part
querb	blir	churp	blork	mart

vert	wirt	yurg	forn	starn
flert	plirg	murph	dorm	charn
twerp	jirm	blurt	chort	carn
pherth	shirp	wurg	tort	plark
merth	blirf	shurst	fort	spart
gerth	mirg	vurn	dorp	bart
perf	dirk	gurn	korsh	blarn
wherx	chirp	burk	forz	sharf
dwerp	nird	glurk	horst	jar

VOWEL DIGRAPH SYLLABLES

feet, meat, key, high, pie, toe, snow, eight, say, mail, moon, soup, stew, cue

bea	foe	migh	woo
bray	stai	shue	beim
slief	wayn	floos	frue
stoy	claut	mayn	wai
phigh	trea	choe	sue
goup	raim	trow	soe
foe	rey	roat	spow
smeed	froak	frail	bleep
quay	shroot	coe	faun
phail	seit	doe	crue
migh	phow	grue	thrail
bleut	grigh	shraw	trow
reap	flail	sawt	trood

DIPHTHONGS

soil, toy, cow, loud, cloud, crowd

moil	floy	fow	ground
roil	spoy	prow	roud

p h o i l   g l o y   c h o w   f r o u n

g r o i n   t r o y   b r o u s   m o u n

t o i n   p h o y   g r o u s   p o u n

CONSONANT - le SYLLABLES

-ble	-cle	-dle	fle
un cle	spin dle	truf fle	muf fle
bu ble	ris cle	sty dle	stu fle
co ble	flun cle	whee dle	tref fle
flo ble	flen cle	fin dle	whif fle
sty ble	ran cle	whin dle	mif fle
ra ble	win cle	ran dle	sty fle
fea ble	fan cle	si dle	snaf fle
re ble	dun cle	ban dle	slif fle
gle ble	run cle	bin dle	quaf fle
shru ble	glan cle	span dle	mir fle
ma ble	flan cle	si dle	lam fle

-gle	-kle	-ple	-tle/-zle
bea gle	spar kle	sta ple	lit tle
flee gle	mer kle	am ple	driz zle
smig gle	fin kle	stam ple	mat tle
mar gle	ran kle	wam ple	ruz zle
spen gle	star kle	ru ple	fit tle
mu gle	fer kle	sem ple	fuz zle
bree gle	mir kle	cris ple	syn tle
thir gle	win kle	lem ple	triz zle

Time: Four Weeks

PLANNING SUGGESTIONS

I. Objectives: Students will understand the meanings of *vowel*, *consonant*, *digraph*, *blend*, *open* and *closed syllables*, *vowel-consonant E syllables*, *R-controlled syllables*, and *consonant-LE syllables*. They will formulate the meanings of these words through the use of a modified concept attainment model, and learn to read and to spell nonsense words with six kinds of syllables. In addition, they will learn how to study and to take notes.

II. Materials: Lists of nonsense words illustrating the six kinds of syllables; description of the SQ3R method of study, and examples of different kinds of note taking.

III. Procedures:

A. Review what had been taught the previous day or week.

B. Students formulate definitions of *vowel*, *consonant*, *digraph*, *blend*, and other syllables from studying examples and nonexamples placed on the blackboard or overhead . Students write their definitions and file them under the Sounds and Symbols section of their notebook.

C. Introduce nonsense words containing the six kinds of syllables with digraphs and blends to read while using a pencil as focus.

D. Dictate nonsense words from the above lists and have students use the S.O.S. technique in spelling the words. Words from the students' texts are also given in dictation.

E. Have students learn how to use the SQ3R method of study. Teach them to survey a chapter in their text, turning statements in bold print into questions, then to read, recite, and review what they have read. Using a chapter in a student text, illustrate the method, and have students read aloud sections of the introduction, topics, subtopics, and summary.

F. Teach students how to take notes. Using newspapers, have students find the *who, what, where, when, why,* and *how* information in articles. They need to learn how to select crucial information from their texts and from lectures, to report main ideas in headline form, to summarize, and to abbreviate their notes. They also learn to use note taking devices such as charts, brief outlines, and "maps." In order to record important facts from lectures, students need to improve their listening skills.

IV. Evaluation: Students' knowledge of definitions such as *vowel, consonant, digraph,* can be tested with oral or written questions, and by having students identify these elements within words. Students' ability to read and to spell nonsense words illustrating the six kinds of syllables is judged by the accuracy of their oral reading, and their spelling of words given in dictation. To evaluate how well students know the SQ3R method of study, have them describe this approach orally or in writing on their "exit" slips (short summaries written at the end of class). To assess how well students are able to take notes, make a small speech and have them note the important facts. In addition, give them an article or a chapter in a text to summarize.

Chapter 5

Syllabication

Once students have mastered basic sounds and symbols, and they appear to be ready to decode polysyllabic words, you may encounter a formidable learning block—a fear of long and difficult-looking words. What most readers take for granted—the facility, in a fraction of time, to see a word in its parts and to pronounce it, even if the meaning is unknown—is a skill that eludes many students with dyslexia. Who can imagine this long-time fear that began, perhaps, when these individuals first realized other students could read what appeared to them to be an impenetrable jungle of letters. At some point, these students may have asked for help, but stopped when they noticed the looks of derision and disbelief on the faces of peers. Then, as self-confidence waned, and they began feeling "stupid," they wanted only to escape attention, focusing on anything rather than reading. Now, as adolescents, they rarely ask questions and have developed patterns of guessing and avoidance. If they are asked to read aloud in a regular class, they may shake their heads and stare numbly at their books.

If any teacher suggests, in front of the class, as many still do, that one of these students get help in a resource class, the student often sits, paralyzed by shame and a sense of inadequacy, wishing to be anywhere in the world but in that classroom. If you are a resource teacher, your role is twofold: you must convince these students that they can learn to read fluently, and that the fear of words can be dispelled. In a "safe" place, where there is no hurt or ridicule, begin by putting ridiculously long words on the blackboard, leaving a small space between syllables, and making a game of having one or two students "gobble" up the syllables (eliminating syllables as soon as they are pronounced). Humor dissipates fear and creates instant rapport. Using humor

57

appropriately, you can make students forget the cycle of failure and become motivated enough to believe that once they learn how to syllabicate words, guessing will no longer be necessary. They will be able to pronounce long and unfamiliar words, and, with practice, increase fluency and comprehension as they read.

In English orthography, there are variations in the way a word is divided into syllables. To preserve the etymological meaning of a word such as *native*, the British divide it as *nat ive* (from the Latin *natus*), although Americans divide the same word phonetically (*na tive*) The same word, however, may be pronounced differently in a variety of English dialects (*The Oxford Companion to the English Language* 1992). In addition, phonetic syllabication is often at variance with the graphic syllabication practice of printers and editors. Therefore, because the rules of syllabication are not fully standardized, show variations in some dictionaries, and do not always correspond to pronunciation, Alice Ansara believed that practice in syllabication must be "simplified in order to ensure rapid word identification" for dyslexic adolescents (*A Guide to the Teaching of Reading* 1966). Because it is imperative that these students learn to read as rapidly as possible, they have no time to struggle with all the rules and exceptions based on accent, spelling, and etymology. Ansara narrowed the ten major rules of syllabication to three, which she thought sufficient. To avoid confusion, these rules must be followed by the student in spite of variant syllabications in the dictionary. Ansara was adamant that students not be given definitions of these rules, but, instead, that they develop understanding of them through examples, questions, discussion, and by writing their own definitions.

Before discussing syllabication rules, be certain that students understand that vowel and consonant digraphs, as well as blends have one sound (see Chapter 4). Then review the concept of the syllable. Ansara outlined a way students could "think" through this concept. Put three words on the blackboard or overhead:

| so | slowly | slowfooted |

Pronounce these words or ask for a volunteer student who will say them. Then ask how the word in the first column is different from those in the second and third. After discussion, put three more words on the blackboard:

| see | settle | settlement |

Follow the same procedure. The words are said aloud; questions are asked; and a discussion ensues. Then add more words to each column:

bat	battle	battlement
tight	tightly	timelessness
great	gainful	gratefulness

If students conclude that the words in the first column have one syllable, the words in the second column, two, and in the third, three, and that a syllable must have a vowel, there are other questions to be asked. Ask how *so*, with one vowel, can have one syllable, and *see*, with two vowels, have one syllable, also? In this way you can also reinforce digraphs and blends. Ansara (1966) believed that if students learn to look carefully at the structure of words, noting similarities and differences, they will begin to perceive that the English language has an understandable pattern and order. When you are assured that students understand the concept of *syllable*, introduce the first rule of syllabication, without stating it.

The first rule of syllable division is division between two consonants that are preceded and followed by a single vowel.

Exercise 1:

Write the following words on the blackboard:

rabbit   tennis   mitten   winter   mascot

After asking students to look at the words and note their similarities and differences, ask volunteer readers to say the words. How many syllables do they hear? When they say "two," say the words again while dividing them between the two consonants:

rab|bit   ten|nis   mit|ten   win|ter   mas|cot

Now ask the students to formulate, in their own words, the first rule of syllable division. If their responses are similar to the above definition, continue to expand the rule by putting more words on the blackboard:

Advil	puppet	despot	until
musket	tender	lesson	temper
mutter	rascal	random	pamper

Ask for volunteers to divide these words, and if they do so correctly, put more complex words on the blackboard:

slapstick   conscience concoction diphthong Ashley

Students note the consonant digraphs, *ck*, *ph*, *th*, *sh*, the vowel digraph *ey*, and the blends *sl*, *st*, and *ct*. More questions and discussion ensue as students are asked to clarify rule one by explaining why they have divided words such as *diphthong* between *ph* and *th*.

Exercise 2

Next, give students lists of VCCV words to read and syllabicate with pencils. When they have read the lists correctly, date and file them in the students' language notebooks.

Exercise 3

Finally, have students prepare notebook pages for dictation by writing *Syllable Division I, VCCV* on the tab in the upper right corner, and *Closed Syllables, Short Vowels* on top of the page. Have them draw lines to make five vertical columns, with the column on the right being widest. (See sample notebook page on page 33.)

Dictate words such as *rabbit*; have the students repeat the word, naming the letters as they write *rab* in the first column, *bit* in the second, and *rabbit* in the fifth column, skipping the third and fourth columns for three-syllable words. Students say the word again as they divide it with a pencil. After writing more VCCV words with two syllables on the blackboard, give a VCCV word with three syllables, *hobgoblin*. If you observe that students are having a harder time with this word, conclude the exercise. During another lesson, and after more practice reading longer and harder words, dictate more VCCV words with three and even four syllables. When presenting the second and third rules, the three exercises listed under the first rule of syllable division should be followed to stimulate critical thinking and provide a multisensory framework for syllabication.

The second rule of syllable division is division after an open vowel and before a single consonant. (See sample notebook page on page 34.)The vowel will usually be long, but may also be short or medial. Ansara recommended that a student try the "long" pronunciation first, and, if that didn't sound right, to try the other sounds. However, because students with dyslexia know little of accent, Ansara wanted them to divide syllables after the vowel to avoid confusion, even though this may not conform to syllable division in the dictionary (1972b).

relay	evoke	aware
bicycle	gyrate	caress
lady	matrix	amend
Malaysia	Godiva	adopt
pagan	cigar	defer
microbe	sliver	salute

The third rule of syllable division separates two vowels that do not form one sound. (See sample notebook on page 35.) The first vowel is usually long and the second one medial (in the middle).

dual	viola	pliable
bias	Thespian	espionage
poet	diurnal	plebeian
duet	viable	incongruity

Having attained some proficiency in learning how to divide words into syllables through penciling, students need to practice syllabicating lists of long and unfamiliar words appended to this chapter. They must persist until, having gained confidence in their decoding, they no longer feel threatened by words.

SYLLABLE DIVISION I (VCCV)

at tack	ap pal	ap pend	al most
of fer	or der	op tic	or bit
hop per	ham mer	hal ter	har ness
dif fer	dim mer	dis gust	dog fish
chat ter	chop ping	clam ber	con dor
con nect	con fess	Cos sack	crab by
Ger man	gos sip	grem lin	gob ble
pal let	pan sy	pas ta	pes ter
er rand	en rich	en trust	ed dy
tat ter	tes ty	thun der	tem per

un bend	un just	ul cer	un lock
rug ged	rum pus	rid den	rus tic
man ner	man tle	mar ket	mar ry
mas ter	mol ten	mut ter	Mon day
fal con	fif ty	flap per	flat ten
in vent	in ject	in fant	in put
les sor	lot to	lit ter	lim ber
scrim mage	scup per	sex tant	ship ping
ten nis	ten don	traf fic	tur nip
rab bit	ran dom	ras cal	rob ber
smat ter	sun set	sum mon	ser mon
nor mal	Nel son	Nes tor	nap kin
muf fin	men tal	mus ket	mit ten
pig ment	pep per	pen cil	pon der
yon der	yam mer	yar row	Yan kee
Vul can	vul gar	ven ter	ver bal
wan ton	wil ful	Wil son	wis dom
bat ter	bub ble	bor der	Bos ton
con vent	con text	cob web	car bon
Den nis	dis turb	dis till	drop let
flat ter	fin ger	fun gus	fun nel
glad den	gas ket	grif fin	gos pel
hap less	hop ping	her mit	hec tic
jet ty	jar gon	jas per	jab ber
ket tle	kit ten	ker nel	kid nap
les son	lad der	len til	lum ber
ab sent	an nex	as sent	as cot
en trap	en gulf	es cape	es cort
os prey	ot ter	ob ject	or der
up per	un der	un rest	un lock
zip per	zir con	Zon ker	zig zag

| thin ning | ther mos | thin ner | shel lac |
| an nul | am nes ty | an ces try | at mos phere |

SYLLABLE DIVISION I (VCCV) (VCCCV)

com mend	com pul sion	com pas sion
dif fuse	dis tinc tion	draf ting
ef fect	em ber	em ploy ment
fil ter	feed back	fin ger tip
Ger man	gin ger bread	ghet to
har vest	help less ness	hob gob lin
jin gle	jit ney	jit ter bug
kip per	kick back	let ter
lin tel	lit mus	lamp post
Man chu	mar ket	mas ter ful
muck rake	mug wump	mis for tune
Nor man	nan ny	con coc tion
pun gent	non con form	non sup port
quick sand	quan tum	ques tion
rud der	rum mage	ruth less
sand blast	sam pan	scaf fold
throt tle	thun der bolt	thy mus
blun der ing	ram part	tres pass
filch ing	dog ged ly	per se vere
sen ti ment	sub sti tute	con di ment
pem mi can	re fur bish	es tab lish
part ner ship	cen sor ship	em bel lish
in trin sic	as sem bly	ac cus tom

SYLLABLE DIVISION II (VCV)

| ti dy | to day | tro phy | ta per |
| a go | a pex | a cute | e lope |

du plex	dri ver	Do lo mites	de pose
e mit	e duce	e ro sion	e va po rate
fro zen	fo cus	fe ver	fa na tic
glu cose	gli der	gro cer	gra vy
ha ven	he ro	ho ri zon	ho ro scope
Ja son	ju bi lee	ju gu lar	ju di cious
ki wi	ko sher	Ko dak	ki mo no
lo tus	lo cal	li ti gious	lu mi nous
mi nor	mi ca	mi cro scope	mi gra tion
o blige	o pal	o pen	o paque
na tal	no ti fy	No vo cain	ni trate
re vel	re vive	ro bot	re la tive
se mi nar	si mu late	si phon	si za ble
tu bu lar	ty rant	ty pi cal	to ken
pro pane	pro per	pro ton	pro li fic
vo tar y	ve nal	wa ver	to tal
gra da tion	gy ro scope	ga zelle	re cum bent
mu ta tion	mu ni tions	mo men tous	mu ti ny
mo no rail	mo no po ly	mo las ses	mo nas tic
tri cy cle	to ta li ty	to po gra phy	te na cious
sa bo tage	spe ci fic	sy nop sis	sa cri fice
clo ver leaf	cu mu lus	co mo tose	ca the dral
vo ca tion	vi va cious	va can cy	va len tine
du pli cate	di ver sion	do mes tic	di vi sion
re ver be rate	ri di cule	rhi ni tis	ri vu let
di ver si ty	du ti ful	dra ma tic	du pli ci ty
a na to my	a go ny	a na lo gy	a qua tic
hy po the sis	hy po der mic	hi ber nate	hi bis cus
e le ment	e rup tion	e me tic	e va sive
a bu sive	a do be	au gu ry	a ban don
o ver flow	o ver whelm	o mis sion	o vu late

re flec tive	re cy cle	re la tion	re clu sion
bo nan za	bo ni to	bla tant	bu co lic
fo ment	fla vor ful	fo cus sing	fi nan cial

SYLLABLE DIVISION III (V/V)

a vi a ry	fo li ate	re im burse	o di ous
sci ence	Si er ra	si es ta	sco li o sis
the a ter	te di ous	ki osk	ka o lin
ob vi ous	hi de ous	qui et	Ro me o
cli ent	hi a tus	o ri ole	ba o bab
Zo di ac	al li ance	al tru ist	po di um
pi o neer	li a ble	jo vi al	gi ant
ge ni al	re in vent	car di ac	pe on y
bi og ra phy	vi o la tion	vi ca ri ous	e go ist
ad ver bi al	vi o lin	di u re tic	di a lect
di o cese	ar du ous	va cu i ty	me di ate
co in cide	mo bi lize	va ri ous	vir tu al
di ag nose	si es ta	va lu a tion	ob vi ate
vi a duct	In di an	bi en ni al	per me ate
al tru ist	pan the on	scor pi on	di a ry
re in force	gra du ate	fu ri ous	me mo ri al
le ni ent	he ro ic	o be di ent	ce re al
sci en tist	o a sis	a re a	Vi et nam
me ni al	mi nu et	mu se um	va ri e ty
sci on	e ven tu al	Vi en na	co op e ra tion
nu cle us	i o dine	nau se a	a li en

WORDS FOR SYLLABICATION

| em bar go | re mem ber | hu mi di ty | fres co |
| in som ni a | Bir ming ham | can di date | crim son |

con fess	con cen trate	pro duc tion	se lect
me te or	sub merge	in con stant	Sa turn
si lent	whis per	re bel	re tro grade
tra gic	de ten tion	po si tion	vo ca tion
do na tion	sa tis fac tion	in no cence	po ver ty
ar tis tic	per so na li ty	wist ful ly	mi ti gate
ac cu mu late	mi to sis	hu mi di ty	at ten tion
com man der	cap tain	mer maid	im pair
spot light	de jec tion	ro ta tion	re ac tion
in tro duce	ma ni fold	ap ti tude	re le vant
de fec tion	con trap tion	in ten tion	at ten tion
dic ta tion	func tion	fric tion	con sent
fab ri cate	ob li gate	hur ri cane	tor na do
en ti ty	ter min al	ven det ta	ra tion
u ti lize	mo no po ly	hos pi tal	di verse
fra ter nal	gla mor ize	con ces sion	pre am ble

R - CONTROLLED SYLLABLES

garrulous	chimerical	corroboration
supercilious	aperture	agglomeration
horticulture	perfunctory	nefarious
equatorial	virtuoso	taciturn
miserable	gregarious	mercenary
correlate	impervious	heresy
exuberance	belligerence	hysterical
omnivorous	adverbial	plagiarism
onerous	hurricane	popular
globular	aromatic	planetary
adulterous	artificial	mysterious
fortunate	puerile	savory

wonderful	monetary	governor
numeral	cavernous	surrender
furniture	turbulent	Churchhill
maturity	ponderous	carnation
Armenian	percussion	permanent
scampering	numbering	pampering
conferring	circumstance	contractor
slippery	personify	flattering
dispersion	oppression	repercussion
muttering	blundering	filtering
prosperous	therapeutic	perspire

VOWEL DIGRAPHS

ai/a/	ay/a/	ea/a/	ey/a/
impair	doomsday	greatness	grey
sailing	playtime	overbearing	convey
retail	payment	breakable	prey
complaint	portray	swearing	purvey
sustain	birthday	wearing	they
fingernail	crayon	tearing	hey
proclaim	Wednesday	steakhouse	survey
scatterbrain	birthday	unbearable	obey
ee/e/	ea/e/	ei/e/	ey/e/
screeching	release	perceive	Charley
discreet	disease	receive	chimney
bleeding	seamstress	ceiling	motley
coffee	underneath	seizure	turkey
esteem	bequeath	protein	valley
absentee	appeasement	conceive	whiskey
tweezers	disappear	deceit	hockey

freezing	arrears	neither	turnkey
steering	demeaning	either	kidney

COMPOUND WORDS

horseback	manmade	earthquake
housewife	blueberry	teamwork
houseboat	football	rainstorm
makeshift	stardust	moonlight
beehive	crabcake	sunshine
shipshape	farmhouse	spaceman
teamwork	snowball	notebook
handrail	turncoat	pinwheel
fanbelt	daydream	mailbox
barnyard	website	toothbrush
railroad	skinhead	skylab
newspaper	stairwell	milkman
football	makeshift	timeline
shoelace	bluebird	bathroom
silkscreen	weekend	upstream
nobody	strawberry	rattlesnake
sailboat	northwest	woodland
cheeseburger	butterfly	grasshopper
limestone	homemade	handmaiden
pinwheel	campfire	starlight
flashlight	plaything	pancake
earthworm	schoolbook	playground
ballgame	bluebird	typewriter
springtime	statesman	summertime

ADJECTIVES

outrageous	wonderful	marvelous	remarkable
salubrious	gracious	spurious	fallacious
advantageous	erroneous	reasonable	shabby
refined	sympathetic	excitable	shady
tedious	wondrous	beautiful	gracious
ephemeral	cosmopolitan	automatic	agreeable
grateful	fortunate	memorable	obsolescent
pathological	tropical	fabulous	incredible
unbelievable	excitable	superstitious	irritable
buoyant	superb	colorful	famous
studious	motivated	haunted	intelligent
apathetic	empathetic	sensitive	acrobatic
artificial	practical	fiftieth	magical
joyous	enjoyable	fabulous	distinguished
vigilant	foolish	immature	picaresque
lustrous	lovable	embattled	geometric
spacious	specious	emotional	candid
youthful	succinct	unique	optimistic
responsible	fictitious	obnoxious	scholarly
tyrannical	divisible	singular	unusual
circuitous	manifold	meticulous	paltry
offensive	obstinate	observable	doubtful
timid	haughty	belligerent	pallid
healthful	deliterious	handsome	homely
audacious	petulant	quarrelsome	placid
profuse	provident	breezy	barbarous
creative	connective	ambiguous	pessimistic
simple	blissful	desperate	childish
victorious	suspicious	miserable	miserly

indigent	wasteful	omnivorous	reserved
bestial	convenient	herbivorous	Hellenic
carnivorous	stupendous	miraculous	winsome
wistful	slender	silky	risible
boastful	impious	restful	troublesome
intrepid	courageous	crispy	fretful
frivolous	frisky	garrulous	fugitive
mordant	meddlesome	misanthropic	peppery
ironic	venomous	poisonous	curative
daring	athletic	murderous	swarthy

VERBS

whistled	pondered	desired	betrayed
considered	decorate	criticize	facilitate
discern	captivate	authorize	prevent
contemplate	enrich	correlate	signify
study	promote	believe	recognize
suggest	destroy	create	discriminate
illustrate	reduce	implore	receive
admit	represent	govern	characterize
communicate	begin	witness	despair
occupy	symbolize	betray	engage
absorb	experience	pacify	aggravate
segregate	sanctified	invalidate	disagree
discover	reproach	disguise	dishonor
negate	burglarize	admire	arise
ratify	reconcile	ramble	develop
overreact	overrun	overshadow	paddle
sympathize	empathize	infiltrate	stultify

ignite	regress	impinge	devour
immerse	refer	paddle	sedate

NOUNS

station	institution	variation	grammar
secretary	inventor	friendship	creator
religion	abstraction	statement	pantheism
flirtation	pilgrimage	symbolism	optician
slavery	achievement	scholar	traitor
recitation	auctioneer	childhood	American
attraction	captain	physician	pension
compassion	government	medicine	astronaut
moratorium	subordination	carpenter	emotion
revision	craftsman	submarine	diplomat
monastery	landscape	automobile	carbon
conversation	concentration	infiltration	omission
adaptation	creation	framework	diversity
whiskers	tension	commune	criteria
pension	thunder	territory	geography
basketry	celebration	poverty	mission
gardener	mythology	condition	traction
commission	frustration	completion	freedom

Time: Three Months or Longer

PLANNING SUGGESTIONS

I. Objectives: Students will understand the concept of *syllable*, and will know how to divide polysyllabic words according to three rules of syllable division. They will also learn how to study for and to take tests.

II. Materials: Lists of polysyllabic words illustrating the three rules of syllable division, and a sample text.

III. Procedures:

A. Continue to work on particular sounds that may be troublesome for students.

B. Put lists of one, two, and three syllable words on the blackboard for students to "think" through and note the number of syllables in words in each list.

C. Introduce words illustrating the first rule of syllable division (division between two consonants preceded and followed by a single vowel), and divide them for students on the blackboard or overhead. After studying enough examples, students formulate the rule. Lists of words are given for reading (using the pencil to divide syllables), and later for dictation using the S.O.S. technique. Students file these lists under the "syllable division" section in their notebooks.

D. When students have mastered the first rule of syllable division, introduce the second rule (division after an open vowel and before a single consonant), and the procedure outlined above is followed. Students continue to read and to spell these words until they master the rule.

E. When students thoroughly understand the second rule, introduce the third rule (division between two vowels that do not make one sound). Again the same procedure is followed with enough syllabication and spelling until students achieve mastery.

F. For reinforcement, continue to give students lists of words with examples of all three rules, and unfamiliar or difficult words from the students' texts, for syllabication and dictation.

G. Students learn how to review class notes and important readings before tests and to bring pens and paper. When given the test, students look it over before answering questions, noting essay questions that will require more time to answer. They know that in true-false questions, the answers must be true or false without exceptions. They work carefully, but as quickly as possible, reading instructions carefully. Students understand the meanings of *define, describe, explain, identify*, and *compare* and *contrast*, and they are careful to answer two-part questions completely. Finally, they check their answers for accuracy.

IV. Evaluation: Assess students on their increased ability to read long and unfamiliar words while dividing syllables with a pencil. Mastery will be evident in their oral reading. The accuracy of spelling from dictation using the S.O.S. technique will also demonstrate mastery. Giving students a sample test with a variety of directions will, in part, reveal how carefully and accurately they take a test.

Chapter 6

Vocabulary

Once students have developed skills in syllabication, it is time for them to begin analyzing words for meaning. Unless they are fortunate enough to have educated parents with extensive vocabularies, who read aloud to them when they were younger, they, like many nonreading students with dyslexia, will lack the vocabulary that avid readers possess. Consequently, by the time these students reach adolescence, their general knowledge will be limited. If they are college bound, they will recognize the urgent need to enlarge their vocabularies to cope successfully with the demands of their studies. According to Alice Ansara (1966), one of the quickest and most effective ways for students to increase vocabulary is by studying Greek, Latin, and Anglo-Saxon roots and affixes. Knowing the roots of words will allow students to understand vocabulary introduced across the curriculum. For example, learning that the Latin root, *duct* means "lead" will help students determine the meaning of *conduction* (science), *production* (geography) or *induce* (English).

Teachers may be surprised to discover that often the very students who are inaccurate readers, have a hard time syllabicating words, and frequently miss small words or parts of words, show amazing interest in learning long and difficult words such as *anthropomorphic*, and in finding more words with the same roots. For other students, with or without reading difficulties, who are accustomed to rote learning, analyzing words can be an arduous task. Here again, one finds validity in Ansara's insistence that for real learning to take place, students must be allowed to discover patterns, rules, and definitions for themselves. Moreover, she believed that by allowing students to supply many of the words that they desire to learn, words from their own experiences, and from their various classes and textbooks, a teacher makes vocabulary activities more relevant.

Give students lists of roots, prefixes, and suffixes, not for memorization, but for syllabication, investigation, and reference. With these lists, students can transfer the root meaning of one word to another, thus expanding their vocabularies. For any discussion of vocabulary, however, students must know the meanings of the following terms:

root   prefix   suffix   assimilation

If you want to assess how much students already know about these terms, simply have them write what they think they know of the definitions the day before you introduce them. Merely asking students for verbal responses is not always wise, since, having heard the terms previously, they may assume they understand the meanings. (If students do know the meanings of the words, give them other related assignments.) Through examples, questions, and discussion students can generate their own definitions. For example, write the word *root* on the blackboard and announce that the class will be searching for the meaning of root. Some students will state that a root is part of a plant; but you can use this interpretation as an analogy for the linguistic term. The root of a plant is buried, sometimes deeply, in the earth. Likewise, students may discover that the roots of certain words are embedded in the past. Put the following word on the board:

unhappy

Pronounce it, then ask what part of the word can be eliminated and what part is essential. Most students will conclude simply by looking at the word, that *un* can be removed, but that *happy* is not only the most important part of the word, it is, in fact, a word. Then put another word on the blackboard.

unhappiness

Again students eliminate word parts attached to the root, *un* and *ness*, and conclude that *happi* is the root. But is it a word? The question then is whether the essential part of a word must always be a word. Present other words.

hemisphere   forgetful   disobey   misuse   overzealous

After these words are scrutinized for essential parts, ask students to define *root*. If their definitions approximate the idea that *a root is a word or part of the word left after all other parts* (affixes) *have been removed*, they are close enough.

Next, introduce the term prefix. Make two columns on the blackboard with *prefix* heading the left column and *root* heading the right. Put the prefixes and roots of the following words in the appropriate columns.

de	face
be	hold
re	act
ex	hale
pre	dict
fore	warn

After questioning and discussion, it should be obvious to students that *a prefix is a part of a word that is placed before the root and alters its meaning*. Tell students that the word itself offers clues to its meaning in that *pre* means before, and *fix* means fixed or fastened.

The notion of assimilation is more complex. Using the same labels, *prefix* and *root*, put the following word parts on the blackboard and pronounce them distinctly:

ad	fair =
ad	sist =
con	mand =
dis	vide =
dis	ficult =
ob	cur =
sub	pend =
sub	fix =
ad	similate =

Ask a student to say *ad fair*. After he says the word, ask him to say it as fast as he can several times. Ask the student what happens to the *d* sound in *ad*? If he understands that it becomes an *f* because the word is then easier to say, proceed to the next prefix and root on the board. It may be harder to explain that the prefix *dis* sometimes drops the *s* or changes the *s* when it assimilates with a root. Finally, discuss *ad similate* which literally means "similar to" or "to make similar," and ask students to write and to share their definitions of assimilation. If they are reasonably close to the following definition, the exercise is concluded. *Assimilation is a process in which the last consonant in a prefix is dropped, or changes to the first letter of the root because of ease in pronunciation.*

Teaching the concept of suffix at this point should not be difficult. Make two more columns on the blackboard, with *root* on the left and *suffix* on the right. Then put these word parts in the correct columns.

doct   or

dent   ist

free   dom:

na   tion

solv   ent

Once more there are questions, discussion, and afterwards students are asked for their definitions, which should resemble this one: *A suffix is a part of a word which comes after the root and which changes its meaning.* Remind students that suffix means *fixed* or fastened under, and, hopefully, they will remember *after* the root.

With their daily work of syllabicating words (always with pencils), word-finding activities, and continuous reading, students may begin to feel more competent and successful in fulfilling their course requirements. In addition, students may also begin to believe, particularly with their burgeoning vocabularies, that going to college is not an impossible goal, and that they can overcome their language difficulties with assistance. (Richards and Romine 1963; Ansara 1966)

USING A DICTIONARY

Anna Gillingham and Bessie Stillman, authors of the seminal text, *Remedial Training for Children with Specific Disability in Reading, Spelling and Penmanship* (1969), described the dictionary as an "indispensable tool" for students with dyslexia. Although some teachers have observed the reluctance of students to use a dictionary, Gillingham and Stillman reported that many of their students regarded the dictionary as a friend. They cautioned, however, that there were essential skills students must possess before they can regard "looking up" words as a pleasurable activity. Though it may be assumed that most adolescents with dyslexia know the alphabet, even if in a slow and halting fashion, a wise teacher cannot take such skills for granted. It is important to assess students' sequencing abilities before beginning a dictionary lesson.

Gillingham and Stillman thought it more appropriate to give adolescents a list of words to alphabetize rather than ask them to recite the alphabet. The suggested list contains words with 1) the initial letters to be sequenced (*cat, house, dog*); 2) the second letter to be sequenced (*blend, brand, bond*); 3) the third letter to be sequenced (*fat, farther, fan*); and 4) the fourth letter to be sequenced (*induce, indirect, indomitable*). It will be obvious how adept students are at sequencing by the amount of time they take completing or not completing the assessment. Continue to give particular students additional help with sequencing, while proceeding with the lesson.

Teach students to recognize guidewords in bold print in the upper right hand corner of a dictionary page. Guidewords indicate the first and last word to be found on a page. If, for instance, a student were searching for the word, *buoy,* he or she might find it on the page between the guidewords, *bunchberry* and *burdensome.* Because most students have developed the habit of searching randomly through pages while looking for words, having them look for guidewords will require repetition and concentration. Students who are having difficulty sequencing will also have difficulty finding a word between guidewords. Now ask the students to write down all the information they find after the word, *buoy.* Discuss what they find and do not find and then go through this word entry more carefully.

Students will find the spelling of the word, *buoy,* in bold print extending slightly into the margin. Words with two or more syllables will show a division. If the word has variant spellings, these will appear next. Ordinarily, however, what follows the spelling of a word is the pronunciation within parentheses: (boo'e, boi). Diacritical marks for vowel sounds are explained in the key at the bottom of the page in some dictionaries. Often, as with *buoy,* there are two (in some cases, more) ways to pronounce the word. After the pronunciation, the word is identified as a part of speech. *Buoy* is a noun, so the abbreviation will be an *n*. It is also a transitive verb (*tr.v*). (Other parts of speech are identified as *adj.* for adjective, *conj.* for conjunction, *adv.* for adverb, *prep.* for preposition, *pron.* for pronoun, and *interj.* for interjection.) After the part of speech, the plural of a noun is listed if it is irregular. The variant meanings of a word follow next, and, in some dictionaries, synonyms and antonyms are included.

At this point, write the word *etymology* on the blackboard before discussing the history of the English language briefly. Beginning with modern English, a Germanic language, trace its development back hundreds of years to the Old English (OE) and Middle English (ME) periods. Continue by discussing the influences of other languages, such as French (Fr.), Latin (Lat.), and finally Indo-European (IE), an ancient language of unknown origin and location. *The Oxford Companion to the English Language* (1992) is a helpful resource for this information.

Ask the students to write down what they think the word *etymology* means. Students then look for the meaning in the dictionary and rewrite the definition in their notebooks. If their definitions are close to *the history of words or word origins*, they are accepted.

Ask the students to find the origin of the word *buoy*. When they find the abbreviation ME and OFr, explain that these abbreviations mean Middle English and Old French and that the symbol < means "derived from." Point out that this section is set off by brackets. Students will find:

> buoy (boo'e, boi)n. 1. A float, often having a bell or light, moored in water as a warning of danger or as a marker for a channel. 2. A device made of cork or other buoyant material for keeping a person afloat. —tr.v. buoyed, buoying, buoys. 1. To mark with or as if with a buoy. 2. To keep afloat. 3. To uplift the spirits of; hearten; good news that buoyed her up.[ME *boie* < OFr.].

This exercise of finding the etymological meaning of words should be a daily one. Individual students can search for the histories of other words.

Your classroom should have sets of dictionaries so that each student has one available for ready use. The dictionary should have print large enough to make word finding easier for students with dyslexia, troubled as they may be by "twisted symbols" (Orton 1937). Etymological entries are essential for students researching the roots and meanings of their language. Graphic appeal, such as pictures, tables, and graphs, also make using the dictionary a pleasurable activity.

DICTIONARY ACTIVITY

Using a dictionary, do the following:

1. **Divide these words into syllables.**

   parsonage _____

   remonstrate _____

   lasso _____

   saxophone _____

2. **Find the pronunciation for the following words.**

   dhoti _____

   geophysics _____

   German _____

   renovation _____

3. **What are the variant spellings of these words.**

   archeology _____

   medieval _____

4. **Find the parts of speech for the following words. Don't use abbreviations,**

   seminary _____

   someday _____

   retrograde _____

   and _____

5. **Find the plurals of these words.**

   analysis _____

   appendix _____

   crisis _____

   moose _____

6. **What is the first meaning of these words.**

    geography _____

    etymology _____

    erudition _____

    NATO _____

7. **Find the etymological meaning of these words.**

    vile _____

    eulogy _____

    scribble _____

    tragedy _____

8. Make up your own dictionary entry which will include: a word divided into syllables; pronunciation; part of speech; at least two definitions; and an etymological entry.

    _____

    _____

    _____

    _____

    _____

    _____

    _____

    _____

    _____

LATIN ROOTS

act, ag, ig - to do, to move

agent

actor

transact

navigation

cap(t), cept, cip, ceiv, ceit - take

capable

capture

deceptive

principal

deceive

capit - head

decapitate

capital

civ, cit - city

civilize

citizen

civility

clam, claim - cry

proclamation

exclaim

reclaim

clud, clus, clos, claus, clois - to shut

exclude

inclusion

closet

claustrophobia

cloister

cord, cour - heart

discord

accord

courage

encourage

cred - to believe

credit

incredible

creed

discredit

credulous

cur, cour - to run

current

excursion

dic(t) - say or speak

dictionary

dictation

prediction

duc(t) - lead

induct

production

aqueduct

fac, fec, fic, fac(t) - make

imperfect

fiction

magnify

counterfeit

fer - bear/carry
ferry
inference
reference

fin - end
finish
infinite
refinement

form - form/shape
reformation
information
misinform

grad, gress - take steps
gradually
progress
regression

spec, spic - look
spectacles
respectable
inspect

vert - turn
inversion
reversion
diversion

mov, mob - move
movement
automobile
immobility

pend, pens - hang/weigh
pendulum
pensive
depend

port - carry
transportation
import
porter

scrib, script - write
scribble
subscription
inscription

spir - breathe
spirit
inspiration
respiration

vid, vis - see
provide
television
visionary

LATIN PREFIXES

in - in, into
introduction
inactive

ob, oc, of, op - against/toward
obstruct

re - again/ back
return
revert

retro - backward
retrogressive

occupy

offer

opposition

per - throughout

perennial

perceptive

post - after

postscript

postgraduate

postmortem

postwar

pre - before

prevent

precede

preview

pro - forward

progress

procrastinate

promotion

pronoun

proceed

proclamation

provision

retrospective

retroactive

retrograde

semi - half

semiannual

semiconscious

sub, suc, suf, sug, sup, sus, - under

subscription

success

suffix

suggestion

suppose

suspension

trans - across

transportation

translate

uni - one

universe

unicorn

unification

unanimous

GREEK ROOTS

arch - rule
architecture
monarch
archeology

anthropo - human
anthropology
philanthropy
anthropomorphic

bibl - book
Biblical
bibliography

bio - life
biology
biography
autobiography

crac/crat - power
democrat
autocrat
plutocrat

dem, demos - people
democracy
demography
demophobia

derm - skin
dermatologist
hypodermic
endoderm

geo - earth
geography
geology
geometry

graph - record,
telegraph
photograph

metr - measure
diameter
metronome
metrics

mono - one
monotone
monotheism
monologue

onym - name
synonym
antonym
homonym

path - feeling.
sympathy
empathy
apathy

phon - hear, sound
phonics
phonology
phonograph

poly - many
polygamy
polysyllabic

psych - mind
psychology
psychopath
psychic

tele - distant
telephone
telescope
telepathy

thermo - heat
thermometer
thermal
thermonuclear

GREEK PREFIXES

a, an - not, without
atheist
amoral
anarchy

antihistamine

apo - away from
apology
apostasy

amphi - both
amphibious
amphitheater
anti - against
anticlimax
antidote
deca - ten
decade
decagram
December
dia - across, apart
diameter
diagonal
diagnosis
dys - bad, difficult
dyspepsia
dyslexia
dysentery
hemi - half
hemisphere
hemiplegia
hyper - over, beyond
hypertension
hypercritical
hyperactivity

apotheosis
cata - completely
catalog
catacombs
cataclysm
catastrophe
hypo - under, deficient
hypodermic
hypoglycemia
hypothesis
hyperbole
meta - change
metaphor
metamorphosis
metabolism
mono - one
monotheism
monochromatic
monarch
pan - all
pantheism
pantomime
panorama

ANGLO-SAXON PREFIXES

a - on, to
aboard
ahead

bedraggled
befriend
by - near to

after - behind/afterwards
afterthought
afterwards
afterglow
be - near to/in addition
belittle
forebear
forehead
forth - forward
forthcoming
forthright
mis - badly
mishandle
mistake
misdoing
misbegotten
misgiving
off - from, away from
offshore
offshoot
out - beyond, outside
outgrow
outmaneuver
outsourcing
over - in excess of/ too much
overabundant

bypassenger
bypass
bygone
byroad
fore - before/in front of
forearm
overflow
overconfident
thorough - completely, pass
thorough
thoroughfare
thoroughbred
thoroughgoing
un - contrary/ removal
unprofessional
unconcerned
unyielding
under - beneath
underwriter
undersigned
with - against
withstand
withdraw
withhold
without
within

ANGLO-SAXON AND LATIN SUFFIXES

Abstract noun suffixes - Act of, state of, condition of

free<u>dom</u>	happi<u>ness</u>	na<u>tion</u>
kingdom	fondness	station
serfdom	joyfulness	correction
martyrdom	playfulness	indication
		condition
state<u>hood</u>	ser<u>vice</u>	deduction
childhood	justice	projection
hardihood	cowardice	sedition
neighborhood		tradition
	partner<u>ship</u>	vocation
govern<u>ment</u>	relationship	duration
resentment	courtship	solution
harassment		destruction
tournament	perform<u>ance</u>	election
	tolerance	rotation
buoy<u>ancy</u>	brilliance	migration
occupancy	dalliance	immigration
hesitancy	acceptance	probation
		reception
effici<u>ency</u>	pati<u>ence</u>	information
persistency	diligence	conservation
fluency	persistence	calculation
dependency	resilience	definition
		redemption
accura<u>cy</u>	national<u>ism</u>	relation
agency	jingoism	fermentation
piracy	mysticism	constellation

perfidy

slav<u>ery</u>

shrubbery

mockery

wid<u>th</u>

growth

dearth

acquitt<u>al</u>

manual

terminal

multi<u>tude</u>

magnitude

fortitude

platitude

socialism

communism

witticism

totalitarianism

egalitarianism

marri<u>age</u>

parsonage

hostage

plent<u>y</u>

insensitivity

rigidity

pict<u>ure</u>

dentures

stricture

nature

commendation

contemplation

expectation

condensation

inva<u>sion</u>

seclusion

supervision

inversion

intrusion

indecision

collision

delusion

subdivision

subversion

precision

television

NOUN SUFFIXES INDICATING DOER OR AGENT

play<u>er</u>

speaker

raider

instruct<u>or</u>

counselor

editor

creditor

professor

sponsor

doctor

auction<u>eer</u>

engineer

charioteer

privateer

artis<u>an</u>

physi<u>cian</u>

guardian

bragg<u>art</u>

dast<u>ard</u>

dent<u>ist</u>

receptionist

botanist

zoologist

orthodontist

microbiologist

endodontist

psychologist

endocrinologist

philanthropist

dermatologist

NOUN SUFFIXES INDICATING DIMINUTIVENESS AND THE FEMININE

din**ette**	part**icle**	suffrag**ette**
rosette	corpuscle	
kitchenette	molecule	prin**cess**
		mistress
executrix	seam**stress**	ancestress
aviatrix		

ADJECTIVE SUFFIXES MEANING *FULL OF, RESEMBLING, HAVING THE NATURE OF, ACTING LIKE,* OR *CAPABLE OF:*

comfort**able**	continu**al**	toler**ant**
likable	natural	brilliant
translatable		
	insul**ar**	confid**ent**
irresist**ible**	globular	imminent
audible		resilient
discernible	mercen**ary**	
		infant**ile**
grace**ful**	agr**arian**	senile
plentiful		fertile
hopeful	trag**ic**	futile
bountiful	frantic	docile
thankful	tactic	mobile
child**ish**	prac**tical**	help**less**
bookish	comical	voiceless
hawkish		childless
mannish	suggest**ive**	friendless
brutish	conducive	cleanliness

kind<u>ly</u>	comparative	graci<u>ous</u>
unsightly	decisive	wondrous
worldly	permissive	fabulous
friendly		credulous
	desult<u>ory</u>	
filth<u>y</u>	dilatory	comat<u>ose</u>
flighty	prohibitory	morose
haughty	congratulatory	
naughty	sensory	
mighty	dilatory	
feisty		

VERB SUFFIXES MEANING *TO MAKE* OR *TO PRACTICE*

elucid<u>ate</u>	broad<u>en</u>
fluctuate	lengthen
concentrate	widen
educate	fallen
separate	risen

SPECIAL COURSE VOCABULARY
English

plot	conflict	dialogue	epiphany
dialect	resolution	metaphor	personification
simile	essay	conjugation	declarative
imperative	exclamatory	interrogative	narration
monologue	glossary	hyperbole	transitive
allegory	conjunction	interjection	adjective
symbolism	dictation	vocabulary	antecedent
subordination	synonym	protagonist	antagonist
participle	homonym	character	antonym

Social Studies

domination	abolition	tariff	expansion
ultimatum	capitalism	communism	medieval
Renaissance	colonialism	topographic	insurrection
armistice	emergence	continent	hemisphere
constitution	nonviolence	segregation	emigration

Science

conservation	classification	thermonuclear	evaporation
microscope	amorphous	herbaceous	equilibrium
synthesize	embryonic	micrometer	photosynthesis
germination	fungicide	transmutation	altimeter
dehydration	conservation	ecology	multicellular
spectroscope	humidity	saturation	oscillation
evaporation	condensation	barometer	centigrade
heterogeneous	sustainability	sedimentary	intermolecular
luminosity	buoyancy	coefficient	equation
taxonomy	meiosis	diatomic	diffusion

Mathematics

trapezoid	triangle	polygon	parallelogram
rectangle	quadrilateral	reciprocal	decimal
theorem	hypotenuse	simultaneous	approximate
concentric	denominator	numerator	vertical
cosine	obtuse	diameter	intersection

Time: Continuing Activity

PLANNING SUGGESTIONS

I. Objective: Students will understand the concepts of *root*, *prefix*, *suffix*, and *assimilation*. They will understand the meaning of some Greek, Latin, and Anglo-Saxon roots and affixes, and realize how knowing these will increase their vocabularies. Students will also become proficient in using the dictionary.

II. Materials: Lists of Latin, Greek, and Anglo-Saxon roots and affixes, and dictionaries.

III. Procedures:

A. Continue work on syllabication, oral reading, and dictation, using the S.O.S. technique.

B. Introduce the concept, *root*, by putting words such as *unhappy*, *misguided*, and *information* on the blackboard or overhead, and having students remove all parts of the words but the essential parts, *happy*, *guide*, and *form*, which are the roots. Introduce prefix by making two columns—prefix and root—and writing *de face*, *be hold*, *fore warn*, until the students understand that a prefix is a part of a word attached before the root, and which alters its meaning. When students have formulated the definitions for root and prefix, introduce *suffix* by making two columns of words, (*doct or*, *dent ist*, *free dom*), under the headings root and suffix. Give enough examples until they discern that a suffix is a part of a word attached after the root. Introduce the concept of *assimilation* by again presenting roots and prefixes. Having students say the prefix *ad* and the root *fair* with increasing rapidity will make them realize that the *d* on *ad* changes to *f* (*af-fair*) because of ease of pronunciation.

C. Students will also learn how to use a dictionary, to become more adept at sequencing, to examine particular words, and to note guidewords, words in bold type, pronunciation, grammar, meaning, and etymology.

D. Students will be given lists of Greek, Latin, and Anglo-Saxon words to read and syllabicate, while using a pencil, and for dictation using the S.O.S. technique.

IV. Evaluation: Students will be given Greek, Latin, and Anglo-Saxon words to identify, and they will be given a written dictionary activity to assess their understanding of word entries in the dictionary.

Chapter 7

Spelling and Word Structure

Although reading fluently and with understanding is the first priority for adolescents with dyslexia, spelling cannot be avoided. Spelling, the encoding of words, is one of the most difficult tasks for students, and one they most want to avoid. For many students, poor spelling is the obvious indication of their language problems, and the source of many critical comments from teachers. Consequently, a large proportion of these students avoid writing tasks and have little hope of ever learning to spell. After language therapy has begun, however, and if you have been dictating words using the Simultaneous Oral Spelling (S.O.S) technique, students may feel more confident about their spelling. If the lists of dictated words in a student's notebook have been reviewed with positive results after one week, and then again after three weeks, he or she may be more confident that correct spelling is an attainable goal.

During the first weeks of language therapy, strive to familiarize students with textbooks, to help them with classroom assignments, and to persuade them that they can learn to read. During these activities, numerous opportunities for spelling remediation occur. A student may ask for assistance in rewriting a paper that is full of misspellings, along with another teacher's comments that accuse the student of careless and indifferent work. After correcting the spelling, show the student words with similar patterns. Later, consult with the student's other teachers to point out that the pattern of misspellings made by the student indicates not carelessness, but a problem with encoding particular sounds.

When evaluating stories and poems, unless they are assignments, commend students for unusual thoughts or unique insights and give positive feedback to encourage expressive writing. Urge students to use all the words in their vocabularies regardless of misspellings.

Adolescents, who often experience conflicts with peers and parents, have much to communicate. Assuage students' fears by telling them that explorers like Lewis and Clark kept fascinating journals in which they referred to "bars" instead of "bears" without having the word circled and the writers reprimanded. Meanwhile, "lift" misspelled words from students' writing and include them in lists for dictation.

Misspelling cannot be ignored, especially if it blocks communication. When students write to each other in class or in other classes, they are strongly motivated to have a teacher help them edit their work. Nancie Atwell (1987) wrote that students can be taught to edit their own work by having them circle words with uncertain spellings and then check the words in a dictionary. Looking up words in a dictionary, unfortunately, may be nearly impossible for students with severe dyslexia, who may lack phonological awareness of word patterns, or who invariably reverse or substitute letters and words. Classroom teachers who provide dictionaries during tests often fail to understand that it is not "laziness" but disability, that keeps certain students from using the dictionary.

After persuading students to write, next persuade them that there are techniques to help them remember the spellings of words. Both you and your students must be patient, however, because years of not hearing sounds correctly, or of not seeing the correct configuration of words makes spelling one of the most difficult language problems to remediate. Fortunately, spell-checks on typewriters and computers can be of great assistance for students with spelling difficulties.

Students have four subdivisions in their notebooks under the spelling category: special categories, nonphonetic words, spelling rules, and dictation. *Special categories* will include words from student texts or assignments, word patterns, vowel digraphs, and homonyms. *Nonphonetic words* ("learned" words) will include any of the 15% of English words that are irregular and/or nonphonetic (Cox 1967). *Spelling rules* will include important rules and generalizations essential for good spelling; and *dictation* will include lists of words from the three subdivisions above, plus any that reflect a student's particular need. For example, in science, students may need to know the definitions and spellings of words such as *biology, geology, astronomy, botany*, and *zoology*. Alice Ansara stated that students learn to spell by knowing the roots of words (Ansara 1977). Accordingly, students learn that *bio* means life, and *logy*, word, speech, or science. You may want to give other examples, *biography*, or *biophysics*, to make students aware of words with the same root. After a discussion of the meanings of assigned and related words, put the words on the blackboard one by one and break them into syllables to aid student pronunciation. After all the words have been seen and pronounced by teacher and students, cover the words on the blackboard and give a pre-test. When the students finish the test, uncover the words on the blackboard so that they can check their own spelling. Discuss the most salient misspellings and then ask students to write the misspelled words several times each and record the spelling of these words in the special categories subdivision of their notebooks.

Note mispronunciations when students read aloud. If a student has trouble reading words such as *frighten, mighty, sight, lighten*, and *blight*, it is unlikely that he or she can spell them. Give this student a list of *igh* words to read at the same time that he or she is underlining the words with a pencil. Later, dictate the same words using the S.O.S. technique. These word pattern problems are also placed in the special category subdivision. Other word patterns that may be troublesome are words that have long *o* sounds such as *scold, mold, fold*, and *embolden*, or long *i* sounds like *kind, pint*, and *wind*.

Words with vowel digraphs (two vowels that make the same sound) are often homonyms, that is, words with the same pronunciation, but with different spellings: *feet* and *feat; blue* and *blew; pear* and *pair;* and *flue* and *flew*. Although these words are short, you will be occasionally surprised to find that students are more likely to spell *periscope* correctly than the homonyms *their* or *there*. Having a quiz game, with contestants giving the appropriate spelling for homonyms in sentences such as "My *feet* hurt," may make students more aware of homonyms. Dictation should follow with phrases such as *"their* friends" or "a *pair* of shoes." Frequent review may be necessary before homonyms are mastered.

Nonphonetic or learned words are irregular words such as *among, friend, although, through, would, could, one, from, enough, aisle, people,* and *any.* Tracing these words on a blackboard, desk, or in sand while saying each letter will help. Having a teacher present the words using the S.O.S. technique, and having students use the words in sentences are also effective ways of learning these difficult words.

Nonphonetic Words

could	although	who
knee	lamb	walk
were	one	once
sure	people	any
through	chalk	says
said	friend	though
was	enough	rough
tough	talk	woman
does	business	laugh
buy	build	beauty
there	thought	from
thorough	move	taught
some	couple	trouble
sugar	foreign	what
caught	honest	none
listen	yacht	trough
love	cough	knife
calf	stalk	

Students need to realize that there are patterns, rules, and generalizations for much of the English language, and a rationale for applying such rules. Alice Ansara noted that even though students have memorized spelling rules, they may not know how, when, or where to use them (Ansara 1977). Inured to failure as they are, students may not be motivated to apply spelling rules. They must be convinced that, in order to improve their spelling, they need to understand how and why adding affixes and letters to words can change the spelling and often, the meanings.

WORD STRUCTURE

Ansara wanted teachers and students to be aware of five levels of word structure, of additions to the roots of words that change meaning. Proceeding from the simple to the complex, they are as follows.

First Level: Adding *s* or *es* to plurals (*trees, horses*); adding *'s* to the singular possessive (*mother's*); adding *ed* and *ing* to past and present participles (*walked* and *talking*); and joining two familiar words in a compound word (*sunstroke*).

Second Level: Adding comparative endings (*small, smaller, smallest*); doubling the final consonant before adding a suffix to protect the vowel (*slipped, shipping, hottest*); and dropping the final *e* before suffixes beginning with *ing* (*making*).

Third Level: Changing words ending with *y* after a consonant before participles and comparatives beginning with a vowel (*babies, cried, happiest*); dropping the final *e* when comparative endings are added (*finer, finest*); adding *y* to make adjectives, and *ly* to make adverbs (*noise, noisy, noisily*); doubling consonants when adding a *y* to protect the short vowel (*sun, sunny*); and using the apostrophe in place of omitted letters (*I've, don't, they're*).

Fourth Level: Forming new words by adding prefixes to familiar roots (*unhappy, unhealthy, disrespect*); and adding simple suffixes (*government, purposeful, tasteless*).

Fifth Level: Syllabication of unknown words; and study of Latin and Greek roots and affixes (Ansara 1966).

Spelling rules and generalizations reflect basic structural changes in words. It would be a mistake, however, to conclude that most students know how and when to make these changes. A reliance on speech is necessary in order to explain why words with the same endings are pronounced differently. However, because of colloquialisms, many students drop the endings of words and may not use plurals or possessives when they speak. Since writing mirrors speech, emphasize pronunciation of word endings, having students form plurals and possessives orally before writing them.

Under generalizations are words with suffixes such as *ous* and *us*; *ful* and *ly*; *cal* and *cle*; *ic* and *ical*; *le* and *el*; and *ance, ant, ence, ent*. Present these words in a logical way that will allow students to deduce, for instance, that words ending in *us* are nouns and those ending in *ous* are adjectives. Dictate the same words using the S.O.S. technique, that is, by saying the word, and by having students repeat the word, naming the letters as they write it, then having them say it again.

For spelling, Alice Ansara (1977) advised teachers to individualize according to need, to proceed from the simple to the complex, to avoid a succession of possibly confusing materials, to refrain from having students memorize rules, and to use multisensory techniques for dictation. Based on these principles, the following procedure is useful for the introduction of each spelling rule.

1. Students formulate the rules through consideration of examples and nonexamples (words that resemble the examples but which lack the essential features for the rule), discussion, questions, and decision making.

2. Students work through a problem-solving chart for each spelling rule.

3. Students apply spelling rules through dictation, using the Simultaneous Oral Spelling (S.O.S.) technique in which students hear a word, repeat it, and write it, while naming each letter, then repeat the word while underlining it with a pencil.

WORDS THAT DOUBLE *F*, *L*, OR *S*, ENDINGS

1) Formulating the Rule

Students are asked to study and compare the characteristics (vowels, consonants, syllables) of words placed on the blackboard beneath the headings, *Examples* and *Nonexamples*.

Examples	Nonexamples
pill	sat
muff	wet
boss	gem
stuff	gag

Pause to let students regard the sets of words, then put more on the blackboard.

brass	tar
smell	web

mess   lad

sniff   lap

When you stop writing words, allow students to study these words, make notes, and discuss their findings with other students. Put two more sets on the blackboard.

loss   jam

gull   fat

After students study these last sets, ask if any individual has formulated a rule about these words. If a student proposes a rule that *words ending in f, l, or s, double the end consonants*, praise the student, but ask if there is any indication that this rule would apply to two and three syllable words? Students study the words again and restate the rule: *words with one syllable with a short vowel double the final consonant if it ends in f, l, or s*. If students are in agreement, have them write the rule in their own words in their notebooks under the subdivision "Spelling Rules."

2) Problem-Solving Chart

Students are now asked to consider whether the following nonsense words double or do not double the final consonants. In the modified chart below, the first example is already completed. Students see the nonsense word, *clif*, and note that it has one syllable, one vowel (V) and ends with one consonant (C). Because the consonant is an *f*, students double it, and form a new word, *cliff*. Students complete the rest of the chart.

WORD	WORD ANALYSIS	SOLUTION	NEW WORD
clif	V + C	double F	cliff
sim	V + C	M does not double	
clas	V + C	double S	class
preet	VV + C	2 V does not double	
muf	V + C	double F	muff
spil	V + C	double L	spill

3) Dictation

If thinking through the chart is not difficult for students, dictate some of the following words using the S.O.S. technique. Stop whenever you observe a student looking hesitant or obviously having trouble spelling a word. Students date their work and file under "Spelling Rules" in their notebook.

gull	boss	press	Tim
spill	smell	when	fret
Sam	bluff	rob	cross
staff	small	blink	swat
nod	prop	pass	stop
bluff	scuff	mud	swell

THE DOUBLING RULE

1) Formulating the Rule

Put the headings, *examples* and *nonexamples* of the doubling rule on the blackboard, letting students study the words, noting similarities, and differences in construction.

Examples	Nonexamples
hop + ed = hopped	sad + ness = sadness
snob + ish = snobbish	cool + er = cooler
snap + ing = snapping	jump + ing = jumping

After questions and discussion, students observe that *hop* is a one-syllable word with one vowel before one consonant, and that if the suffix *ed* were added, the vowel would become long, *hoped*. Therefore, to protect the short *o* sound, the consonant is doubled and the word becomes *hopped*. In the word *sad*, the consonant does not double because the suffix begins with a consonant: *cool* does not double because the consonant is preceded by two vowels; and *jump* does not double because the vowel is followed by two consonants. Present more examples and nonexamples.

mop + ing = mopping	blink + ing = blinking
rip + ing = ripping	tear + ing = tearing

After discussion, write more words; but now ask students to decide under which heading to place the word, and how to determine the spellings of the new words.

drop + ing, seem + ed, flat + ly, hat + ful, red + ish.

If these words are placed and spelled correctly, ask students to write the doubling rule. If one or more students appear uncertain, continue to give examples. If the rule that they write is similar to *words with one syllable that end with one consonant preceded by one vowel, double the consonant if the suffix begins with a vowel*, then students record it in their own words in their notebooks under spelling rules.

If there is time, and to be certain that all students understand, ask individuals to explain the doubling rule using specific roots and suffixes. Having students tell why they are doubling or not doubling is a very important step.

brim + ful = brimful

A student explains that although the word has one syllable, one vowel, and ends with a consonant, the word is not doubled because the suffix starts with a consonant.

2) Problem Solving Chart

When you are assured that students understand the rule, give them the chart created by Alice Ansara (1977) (see page 106). Students apply the doubling rule and give reasons for their decisions. For example, in an analysis of the root *bat*, which is to be joined to the suffix, *ing*, students conclude that *bat* is a one-syllable word, has one vowel (V), ends in one consonant (C), and the suffix begins with a vowel (VC+V). Therefore, to "protect" the short (sh) vowel sound, students solve this "problem" by doubling the consonant, and hence, forming a new word, *batting*. The word, *hand*, however, ends in two consonants, and the suffix, *ful* begins with a consonant, so the word is "O.K." The root and suffix can be combined and doubling is not necessary.

WORD	SUFFIX	ANALYSIS	PROBLEM	SOLUTION	NEW WORD
bat	ing	VC + V	protect sh. V	double C	batting
hand	ful	VCC + C	O.K.	add suff.	handful
mop	ing	VC + V	protect sh. V	double C	mopping
dream	ing	VVC + V.	O.K.	add suff.	dreaming

Additional problem solving charts are included for student practice. After corrections are made, these should be filed in the students' notebooks.

Doubling Rule Worksheet					
word	suffix	word analysis	problem	solution	new word
hop	ing	VC + V	protect short V	double C	hopping
chant	ing	VCC + V	O.K.	add suffix	chanting
slip	ing				
seem	ed				
whip	ing				
clean	able				
rig	ing				
bank	ing				
slop	y				
rest	ful				
mat	ed				
sand	ed				
big	ness				
rap	ing				
sing	ing				
sun	y				
flap	er				
hug	ing				
tear	ing				
fit	ed				

3) Words for Dictation

After students have received sufficient practice working through the doubling process, dictate words that are examples or nonexamples of the doubling rule. Do this by using the S.O.S. approach previously described on page 13.

thinner	fatter	flapper
rubbing	tripped	biggest

snobbish	baggy	warlike
bigness	leafy	walking
flatten	foolish	plodding
trimmed	scanning	helpful
foggy	gotten	runner
passing	sunny	hardest
slammed	dimmer	dimming
jogged	winning	painful
planned	stirred	muddy
spinning	meanness	dirty
mouthful	padded	sloppy

THE SILENT - E RULE

1) Formulating the Rule

Write words on the blackboard that illustrate this spelling rule to elicit discussion and questions. Allow time for students to formulate the rule for themselves.

Examples	Nonexamples
tune + ing = tuning	like + ly = likely
hope + ed = hoped	like + able = likeable
tire + ed = tired	hope + less = hopeless

Students study the examples and nonexamples, comparing features and noting differences. Wait a few minutes, then put more sets on the blackboard.

ride + er = rider	sure + ly = surely
rove + ing = roving	lone + some = lonesome
fame + ous = famous	excite + ment = excitement

(Though more sets may not be necessary, the following can be used if needed).

expense + ive = expensive	complete + ness = completeness
shade + y = shady	improve + ment = improvement
guide + ance = guidance	tune + ful = tuneful

plane + ed = planed	improve + ment = improvement
flake + ing = flaking	use + ful = useful
impede + ing = impeding	trouble + some = troublesome
trade + ing = trading	life + less = lifeless
move + ing = moving	love + ly = lovely
abuse + ing = abusing	lone + some = lonesome
bide + ing = biding	lame + ly = lamely
slime + y = slimy	engage + ment = engagement

Students compare the features of these sets. They may consult with a partner or small group. In examples such as *rider* (*ride + er*), the *e* is dropped because it is not necessary to keep the vowel long. In nonexamples such as *lonesome* (*lone + some*), the *e* is retained to protect the long *o* sound, and because the suffix starts with a consonant. Before students offer a rule, ask them to place other words under the two headings, adding suffixes. They can make decisions individually or in small groups.

shine + y = shiny	late + ness = lateness
fine + er = finer	grate + ful = grateful
wake + ing = waking	care + less = careless
fame + ous = famous	tire + some = tiresome
wade + ed = waded	name + less = nameless

After placing the words, and adding the suffixes, students offer a definition of the silent *e* rule which should be similar to this: *The e is dropped before a suffix that begins with a vowel, but is not dropped before a suffix beginning with a consonant.* Using their own words, students record the rule in their notebooks. They are now ready to apply the rule.

2) Problem-Solving Chart

Students now begin the work of thinking through the process of adding or dropping the silent *e*. In the first word, *debate*, for example, the *e* is dropped before a suffix that begins with a vowel (*ing*) (E +V). Two vowels are unnecessary for keeping the long *a* sound in debate, so the new word becomes *debating*.(See chart on page 109).

Silent E Rule Worksheet					
word	suffix	word analysis	problem	solution	new word
like	able	VCE + V	2 vowels	drop E	likable
dive	ing	VCE + V	2 vowels	drop E	driving
like	ness	VCE + C	O.K.	add suffix	likeness
late	er				
erase	ed				
case	ment				
shine	y				
active	ly				
like	ly				
bake	ing				
ice	y				
awe	ful				
shape	ly				
skate	ing				
wake	ful				
late	ness				
write	ing				
slime	y				
drive	ing				
wade	ing				

WORD	SUFFIX	ANALYSIS	PROBLEM	SOLUTION	NEW WORD
debate	ing	VCE + V	2 vowels	drop E	debating
time	ly	VCE + C	O.K.	add suffix	timely
wake	ful	VCE + C	O.K.	add suffix	wakeful
take	ing	VCE + C	2 vowels	drop E	taking

If students complete their problem-solving chart with understanding, give them some words for dictation. If students need more time to think through the E Rule, postpone dictation and give more problem-solving examples.

3) Words for Dictation

When you are satisfied that students understand the Silent E Rule, begin dictating words using the S.O.S technique. Stop dictating when students seem perplexed by the spelling and review the Silent E Rule before resuming dictation. Remind students to date their work.

tiresome	raked	shining	typing
shaped	rarely	endurance	scaring
officer	manager	valuable	storage
shameless	grateful	placement	shapely
blazing	icy	driver	poker
likeness	notable	homeless	stored
tuning	namely	awful	smoky
bravely	retirement	agreement	preparing
sharing	described	advisable	amusement
refused	truly	shameless	

4) Exceptions to the Silent E Rule

Students should already be familiar with the rule that if *c* and *g* are followed by *e*, *i*, or *y*, the *c* and *g* are usually soft, but if the *c* and *g* are followed by *a*, *o*, or *u*, the *c* and *g* are usually hard. Review this rule to be certain students understand it and can pronounce words such as the following:

regulate	reciprocate	location	register	cutlery
Gandolf	cistern	suggest	culinary	

In the *Silent E Rule, the e is dropped before suffixes that begin with vowels, but is retained before suffixes beginning with consonants.* There are exceptions to the Silent E Rule, however. There are words derived from Middle English, and before that, Old French and Latin, that end in *ce* and *ge*. To keep the *c* and *g* soft in these words, the *e* is retained before suffixes beginning with *a* or *o*. To illustrate these exceptions to the Silent E Rule, put the following words on the blackboard under the headings, *examples* and *nonexamples*.

Examples	Nonexamples
change + able = changeable	change + ing = changing
trace + able = tracing	trace + ed = traced
courage + ous = courageous	encourage + ed = encouraged
pronounce + able = pronounceable	pronounce + ed = pronounced

Students study these words, as you put more examples on the blackboard.

service + able = serviceable   service + ing = servicing

outrage + ous = outrageous   outrage + ed = outraged

Students observe that the *e* is retained in *serviceable* because if it were not, the word would be pronounced with a hard *c* (ser′ vik a bul). In the word, *servicing* (ser′ vis ing), however, the *e* is not needed since the *i* keeps the *c* soft. The students have a definition. *To keep the* c *and* g *soft before suffixes that begin with* a *or* o, *the* e *is retained.*

Knowing the rules is not enough to make students confident spellers. They must know words so well that when they are writing, they will not have to pause frequently to wonder whether they have spelled particular words correctly. Dictation, using the S.O.S. technique, will certainly help, but having students make up and memorize phrases for dictation illustrating these exceptions, will help even more.

What is courageous seems often outrageous and not advantageous.

PLURALS

Most nouns form plurals by adding *s* to the singular.

house - houses, sister - sisters, cat - cats, lake - lakes, chair - chairs, thought - thoughts

Nouns ending in *s, z, x, ch,* or *sh* form the plural by adding *es* to the singular.

kisses	quizzes	boxes	benches	slashes
classes	waltzes	axes	matches	brushes
dresses	buzzes	taxes	churches	clashes
grasses	fizzes	prefixes	witches	wishes

Nouns ending in *y* after a vowel add an *s* to form the plural.

boys	relays	trays	toys	turkeys
rays	chimneys	journeys	valleys	donkeys

Nouns ending in *y* after a consonant change *y* to *i* and add *es*.

ladies	cities	candies	puppies	countries
enemies	stories	spies	libraries	parties

THE Y RULE

1) Formulating the Rule

Introduce this rule by putting examples and nonexamples on the blackboard.

Examples	Nonexamples
happy + ness = happiness	enjoy + ing = enjoying
merry + ment = merriment	monkey + s = monkeys
holy + er = holier	obey + ing = obeying
early + er = earlier	donkey + s = donkeys
carry + er = carrier	decay + ing = decaying
mercy + ful = merciful	obey + ed = obeyed
industry + al = industrial	dismay + ed = dismayed

Students study these words and make conjectures about the difference between the examples and nonexamples. Put more sets on the blackboard.

multiply + er = multiplier	survey + ing = surveying
stormy + est = stormiest	display + ing = displaying
reply + ed = replied	bray + ing = braying

Continue with illustrations until students eventually conclude that, *words ending in y, preceded by a consonant, change the y to i when adding a suffix, unless the suffix starts with i.* Students write the rule in their own words in their notebooks.

2) Problem-Solving Chart

After writing the Y Rule, students apply it. A suffix, *ed*, is added to the word *delay* and to keep the identity of the vowel digraph *ay*, the new word becomes *delayed*.

Y Rule Worksheet					
word	suffix	word analysis	problem	solution	new word
carry	ing	CV + suffix begin. with i	y must remain	keep y, add suffix	carrying
fry	ed	CV + suffix	change y	y changes to i	fried
bury	al				
lovely	er				
busy	er				
enjoy	ed				
ready	ly				
defy	ed				
worry	ing				
hurry	ing				
modify	ing				
study	ous				
lonely	ness				
fly	ing				
heavy	ly				
study	ing				
greedy	er				
sleepy	er				
copy	ing				
beauty	ful				

WORD	SUFFIX	ANALYSIS	PROBLEM	SOLUTION	NEW WORD
delay	ed	VV+ suff	ay keeps ident.	no change	delayed
joy	ful	VV+suff	oy keeps ident	no change	joyful
carry	ing	CV+suff. beg. with i	y must remain	keep y, add suff.	carrying
hurry	ing	CV+suff. beg. with i	y must remain	keep y, add suff.	hurrying
deny	al	CV+suff	change y	y changes to i	denial

3) Dictation

buying	kindliness	heavily	loneliness
delaying	studious	shyly	busier
happiness	modified	delayed	mislaid
supplied	lovelier	cried	decaying
employed	buyer	victorious	occupying
industrious	likely	mysterious	weariness
enemies	crazier	jellies	berries
pitiful	forties	fancies	factories
marriage	replying	funnier	memories

Plurals of nouns ending in *o* and *f* and *fe*

Nouns ending in *o* after a vowel form plurals by adding *s*.

radios   studios   rodeos   cameos   ratios

Nouns ending in *o* after a consonant sometimes form plurals by adding *s* or *es*. Advise students to consult a dictionary or to memorize some of the nouns that end in *es*.

echoes   potatoes   heroes   tomatoes   vetoes

Musical terms of Italian derivation, and words of Spanish derivation add s only.

cellos   pianos   altos   burros   pueblos

Nouns with final *f* or *fe* are derived from Old English and form plurals by adding *s*, by dropping the *f* and adding *ves*, or by having both plurals.

cliffs   staffs   dwarfs   strifes

elves   halves   lives   wives   wolves

scarfs/scarves   roofs/rooves   hoofs/hooves

POSSESSIVES

To show singular possession, write the singular noun first and then add 's. To show plural possession, write the plural noun first, then add an 's or simply add an apostrophe.

Singular	Singular Possessive	Plural	Plural Possessive
friend	a **friend's** book	friends	**friends'** books
girl	a **girl's** dream	girls	the **girls'** dreams
wife	his **wife's** car	wives	their **wives'** cars
mother	my **mother's** diary	mothers	their **mothers'** diaries
horse	a **horse's** hoof	horses	the **horses'** hoofs
giraffe	a **giraffe's** neck	giraffes	**giraffes'** necks
dragon	the **dragon's** teeth	dragons	many **dragons'** teeth
driver	a **driver's** fear	drivers	**drivers'** fears
puppy	a **puppy's** bone	puppies	the **puppies'** bones
thief	a **thief's** loot	thieves	the **thieves'** loot

IE and *EI*

As students study the *ie* and *ei* digraphs placed in these two columns, students should be able to formulate a rule.

ie /e/	ei /e/
field	conceive
piece	receive
shield	deceive
niece	perceive

retrieve	conceit
believe	deceit
relief	receipt

Students will conclude that *ei* comes after the consonant *c*. There are exceptions: words with *eigh* and *ei* that have a long *a* sound.

ei (gh) /a/	**ei** /a/
eight	vein
neighbor	heir
their	skein
weigh	reign
freight	rein

ck and k

Generally, use *ck* after short vowels, and *k* after consonants or other vowels.

hack	chicken	basking	blink
track	Jack	musket	frisk
smack	crackers	sake	snake
peck	tack	tank	hulk
mock	clock	cook	yank
flock	pick	dusk	brook
bucket	pickle	fake	beak
truck	lipstick	trinket	sink
track	hemlock	flank	drink
hammock	mattock	Frank	frisk
derrick	haddock	plunk	anklet
paddock	attack	sulky	napkin
struck	stock	inkling	skulk
ransack	fetlock	squeak	gasket
snack	black	tweak	flask

dge and ge

In general, use *dge* after a short vowel and *ge* after consonants or two vowels.

bridge	fudge	huge	singe
ledge	midget	range	merge
lodging	nudge	strange	gouge
wedge	dodge	charge	large
drudge	ridge	plunge	siege
gadget	cartridge	barge	scourge
grudge	badge	cringe	urge
budget	partridge	binge	wage
midge	sedge	fringe	rage

tch and ch

Usually, use *tch* after a short vowel and *ch* after a consonant or two vowels.

clutch	stitch	pinch	porch
stretch	pitcher	slouch	reach
notch	pitch	couch	inch
witch	hatch	bench	beach
kitchen	butcher	ranch	each
ditch	fetch	henchman	peach
batch	retch	cinch	teach
itch	glitch	hunch	gulch

us and ous

Us is usually a noun ending and *ous* is usually an adjective ending.

crocus	marvelous	tremendous
octopus	famous	stupendous
bonus	nervous	nitrous

exodus	joyous	ludicrous
stimulus	thunderous	ominous
focus	continuous	vigorous
omnibus	humorous	enormous
genius	numerous	strenuous

Past Tense

To add the suffix *ed* to show past tense, students need a knowledge of spelling rules (*f, l, s* and silent-*e* rules).

ed /ed/	ed /d/	ed /t/
scolded	begged	baked
noted	dived	hoped
potted	rigged	liked
waded	tired	skipped
plotted	skinned	danced
nodded	planned	hiked
prided	closed	dropped
faded	named	

THE DOUBLING RULE WITH TWO-SYLLABLE WORDS

1) Accent in Formulating the Rule

Alice Ansara thought this rule should be presented last because of the difficulty students with dyslexia have in hearing and understanding accent in words. A teacher might be advised to introduce this rule slowly, after daily accent-finding exercises. When applying the doubling rule to words with two syllables, students must understand accent or stress, which is emphasis on a spoken syllable or word. About 50% of the English language is derived from Latin, and 10 to 12% from Anglo-Saxon. The words from both languages have similar accent patterns. Latin words are likely to have a prefix, root, and suffix. The prefix is a preposition; the root is the most important part of the word because it supplies meaning; and suffixes show parts of speech. For example, the suffix *-ive* (*active*) indicates that a word is an adjective. In a word such as *active*, with only a root and a suffix, the accent is on the first syllable (ak'tiv). If a word has only a prefix and a root (*resist*), the accent will be on the root (ri zist'). If there are two syllables in the root (*navigate*), the first syllable is accented (nav'i gat). Anglo-Saxon words (*helpful, kingdom, beginning, forgotten*) have accents similar to Latin words (Steere et al.1971).

It is important to introduce the idea of accent orally with a variety of words, asking students to indicate which syllable is stressed in the words that you and the students pronounce in an exaggerated way. Making a game of accent placing, by having students vie with one another to answer correctly, may make this learning less onerous and more pleasurable. Not until all students demonstrate that they can identify accented syllables, should they attempt to locate accent in lists of words. Otherwise, if you try to combine the teaching of accent with the teaching of the doubling rule for two-syllable words, students may become quite confused. If students are in doubt about where the accent is placed in particular words, encourage and help them find the pronunciation of a word in the dictionary. Because the concept of accent is hard for these students to grasp, only the primary accent is identified. When confident that all students know how to determine accent, supply them with words for practice. All words are pronounced before students begin work.

adhere'	forbid'	reduce'
around'	implore'	concur'
withstand'	predict'	return'
omit'	construct'	include'

When students are ready to study examples of the doubling rule in two-syllable words, ask them to repeat the words after you and to place accent marks on both examples and nonexamples on the blackboard.

Examples	Nonexamples
omit' + ed = omitted	num'ber + ed = numbered
forget' + ing = forgetting	await' + ing = awaiting
regret' + able = regrettable	sum'mon + ed = summoned
permit' + ed = permitted	hon'or + ing = honoring
excel' + ing = excelling	afford' + ed = afforded

Next, ask students to study and to compare examples and nonexamples. Write and pronounce more sets of words.

compel' + ing = compelling   retain' + able = retainable

deter'+ ed = deterred   restrain' + ed = restrained

After discussion, students agree that words such as *omit*, which ends in one consonant preceded by one vowel, double when the accent is on the root, which ends in one consonant preceded by one vowel; but in words with two-syllable roots such as *number*, the accent is on the first syllable, and the final consonant does not double. In words used as nonexamples, such as *afford*, the final consonant does not double because it is preceded by a consonant. In *await*, the final consonant does not double because it is preceded by two vowels. After more sets of examples and nonexamples have been discussed, students agree that *two-syllable words that end with single consonants preceded by single vowels, double the consonants before suffixes beginning with vowels, if the accent is on the last syllable of the word* (Steere et al. 1971).

2) Problem-Solving Chart

Students now do their own analysis of two-syllable words for the doubling rule. Before they begin, however, help them place accent marks on the words by pronouncing them. Together, analyze *submit' + ing* (VC+V) and decide that in order to protect the short *i* sound, the consonant (C) must be doubled (*submitting*), possible because the accent is on the second syllable.

WORD	SUFFIX	ANALYSIS	PROBLEM	SOLUTION	NEW WORD
submit'	ing	VC+V	protect sh. V	double C	submitting
reject'	ing	VCC +V	O.K.	add suff.	rejecting
omit'	ed	VC +V	protect sh. V	double C	omitted
lim'it	ing	VC+V	O.K.	add suff.	limiting

Ask students again to observe that consonants are doubled in *submitting* and *omitted* because the accent is on the second syllable. In order to reinforce this concept, give students additional words on which to place the accent, then add a suffix.

trans mit'	+ ing	transmitting____
oc cur	+ ing	_____
re pel	+ ed	_____

for bid	+ ing	_____
pro test	+ ing	_____
for get	+ able	_____
ex cel	+ ent	_____
ad mit	+ ing	_____
con trol	+ ed	_____

3) Words for Dictation:

Using the S.O.S. technique, dictate some of the following words. Dictate a few words each day, but remind students to date each group of words and to file the words under the spelling rules section in their notebooks.

beginning	selected	shorten	harmful
forgetful	compelled	buttoned	repelled
committed	predicting	appearing	happening
opened	contractable	visiting	restrained
submitted	staggered	slandering	shivering
submitted	galloping	recurring	concurred
permitted	transmitted	controlled	rejecting
predictable	expendable	bantering	blistered
crediting	inducted	transportable	describing

Remember that all students with dyslexia may not need all the rules and generalizations presented in this chapter. Only by focusing on individual needs can spelling deficits be overcome. Students with persisent spelling problems need daily dictation until they feel able to write without fear of constant mis-spellings. Meanwhile, students will move into a critical phase of reading—phrasing.

Time: As Long as It Takes

PLANNING SUGGESTIONS

I. Objectives: Students will improve their spelling by understanding and applying spelling rules, and by using a multisensory approach to spell words with patterns, nonphonetic words, and special category words. Students will also understand the meaning of word structure.

II. Materials: Student notebooks, work sheets for the three spelling rules, and lists of words for dictation as well as "Problem Solving Charts," and illustrations of word structure prepared for blackboard or overhead.

III. Procedures:

A. Students continue to read, syllabicate, and spell words with Latin, Greek, and Anglo-Saxon roots and affixes, and to practice oral reading from texts.

B. Students are given difficult, nonphonetic words (*enough, foreign*) to trace as well as to spell, using the S.O.S. technique.

C. They will use the S.O.S. technique to spell words from their texts, words with special patterns, vowel digraphs, and homonyms.

D. Before beginning spelling rules, discuss word structure, and provide many examples of additions to the roots of words that change meaning.

E. Beginning with the F, L, S Rule, present students with examples of one-syllable words ending in a consonant preceded by a short vowel that double the last consonant (*sniff, loss, gull*), and nonexamples such as *prim, lap, jam, flat*. With more examples, students will conclude that one-syllable words that end in *f, l,* or *s* preceded by one short vowel double the last consonant. Give these words in dictation using the S.O.S. technique.

F. Introduce students to the Doubling, Silent-E, and V Rules following the same procedures. Present examples and nonexamples, until they formulate the rule. Then give them problem solving charts that test their understanding and ability to apply the rule. After students demonstrate understanding of the rule, give words in dictation that illustrate the rule, using the S.O.S. technique. As Alice Ansara would have advised, proceed as quickly as possible, but as slowly as you must. Have students file dictation in their notebooks under the "spelling" section.

IV. Evaluation: Students will be given a spelling test that will include nonphonetic words, words with vowel digraphs, words that conform to general patterns such as *ous* and *us*, and words representing the three major spelling rules. Students will also explain the meaning of *word structure* and be asked to give at least four examples.

Chapter 8

Phrasing:
The Next Stage
of Reading

Although teachers often think reading goals are accomplished when students are able to syllabicate and spell words with some facility, it is a mistaken assumption. Students may persist in reading word-by-word, often pausing to reread passages just read in order to analyze the meaning. Just as an infant does not move ordinarily from creeping to standing without learning to crawl, students cannot proceed from word-by-word reading to the fluent reading of passages, paragraphs, essays, and books, without first learning to read in phrases. Only when students begin to read in phrases can they begin to anticipate meaning and author's intent. By reading in phrases, a student "not only understands what he has read but remembers it as well" (Ansara 1972b, p. 131).

Perhaps the most neglected phase of reading—phrasing, and its essential transitional role—was long recognized by Alice Ansara. Her teaching and writing on the importance of signal words and phrasing are a vital part of her work. Of special concern were students, always behind in reading assignments, who read word-by-word in this pattern:

The narrow brown shape of the snake resembling a stick moved in wavelike motion through the water towards the river bank.

The narrow what? Ribbon? Cord? Stripes? No image or anticipation is conveyed. *The narrow brown*, again what? Ribbon?

Cord? Stripes? *The narrow brown shape* may evoke enough interest for students to make them look ahead for the identity of the
shape. But if the students were reading in phrases, they would
read *The narrow brown shape* as a unit, and move ahead quickly
to the snake, sustaining interest in where the snake is going and
what is going to happen. The sentence should be read, not in
twenty-one words, but in no more than six phrases (1966).

The narrow brown shape   of the snake   resembling a
stick moved in wavelike motion   through the water   toward
the river bank.

Ansara (1977) urged teachers to be certain students could
hear phrases and identify them as groups of words attached to
an independent clause. Ask students to complete the following
phrases orally.

Risking his life . . . .

On her way to school . . . .

Eating chocolate . . . .

Running from the wild dogs . . . .

The ancient vase . . . .

Wandering through the swamp . . . .

Learning to use a computer . . . .

Finding information on the Internet . . . .

The high speed chase . . . .

Her attitude. . . . .

Using an overhead projector, have students observe and
read the following sentences in which phrases are clearly sepa-
rated from the independent clause.

A bomb blast   leveled a hotel   in Northern Ireland.

Read the sentence, then ask students to consider which
words are essential in the sentence. Then give more examples:

After the election,   voters held a celebration.

To end years of fighting,   the assembly urged peace talks.

Although she had six children at home   Bridgett Murphy
accepted a position   in the new government.

Mrs. Murphy,   well known   for feeding the poor   in the slums of Belfast,   has her own peace plan.

Again, ask students to state what words in the above sentences are crucial and what groups of words merely add more information. Continue this exercise until you are assured that all students can isolate main clauses from phrases and dependent clauses.

Next, write a simple sentence on the blackboard and give a notecard with a phrase written on it to each of four students.

Jerry's hair turned green.

Ask the students, one by one, to add their phrases to this sentence. The second, third, and fourth students may switch the phrase position of the person who came before them until the sentence makes sense.

After washing his hair   and adding dye   given to him by a friend,   Jerry's hair turned green.

If the sentence is jumbled by the students, ask other students to rearrange the phrases.

Given to him   Jerry's hair   turned green   by a friend and adding dye   after washing his hair.

Although this exercise may be difficult initially, it allows students to see phrases and to think about the positions of phrases in a sentence.

Ansara did not always use the term *phrase* in the strictest sense, that is, a group of words without subject or verb, but more in terms of related units of words dependent on an independent clause in a sentence. At this point, you will want to know whether students understand the distinction between a sentence and a phrase or dependent clause. Using an overhead projector, display a chart with two simple sentences under the word *sentence*, and two phrases under the word, *other*.

sentence	other
John won a ticket to Disneyland.	A ticket to Disneyland.
Mary bought a new bassoon.	A new bassoon.

Ask the students to compare the differences between the two sets. After a few minutes, show two more sets:

sentence	other
The President made a trip to Russia.	A trip to Russia.
Tigers are an endangered species.	An endangered species.

Students again compare these two sets. After allowing students to discuss the differences among themselves, present two more sets. Ask students to discuss their findings. If they have concluded that each sentence has more words than the group of words under *other*, ask one or more students to list the extra words in the sentences on the blackboard. After students have put words such as *John, made, Mary, won, the, President, tigers,* make two new headings on the blackboard, *verbs* and *other words*. Put two sets underneath the headings and ask students to study the characteristics of each set.

verbs	other words
won	the
made	tigers
bought	President
are	Mary

If students are still hesitant and unclear about the differences, add more sets.

concentrate	and
sing	them

Students compare the sets and someone defines a verb as a word that shows action or makes the subject "do something." Ask the students why a verb is essential for a sentence, and a student might say that a sentence must have a verb in order to "make sense" or to express a complete thought. If the students agree on this definition of a sentence, they record it in their notebooks. The next day, perhaps, begin again by displaying more prepared sets for presentation on the overhead.

Introduce dependent clauses by first asking students to think about what it means to be dependent on another person. After discussion, and without having given away the definition, put dependent clauses and nondependent clauses on the blackboard.

Dependent clauses	Other
Although the man stood up,	The oldest daughter was a plumber.
Even though he was her brother,	There was a raging storm outside.

Ask students to compare the two sets quietly for a few minutes and then put up two more sets.

Dependent clauses	Other
After he ate fourteen hamburgers,	Wolves are devoted to their cubs.
Although she tried on each dress twice,	Beowulf was a hero.

Now ask students to discuss the differences between the two sets. If a student offers a definition stating that dependent clauses are not complete in themselves, that there is more information needed to make them sentences, ask if others concur with this definition. If the other students are in agreement, re-state the student's definition and ask that the students record it in their own notebooks. If, however, a number of students disagree, continue with other examples and nonexamples or other strategies until the concept is understood. Students may also be asked what an independent clause or sentence is, and, if by this time, only two students understand the meaning of a sentence, have these two students present examples and nonexamples of sentences to the rest of the class. Students need to understand that *a phrase is a group of words,* and that *a dependent clause has a subject and a verb, but does not express a complete thought like an independent clause or sentence.*

Again, when students begin to read in phrases, Ansara noted that they are taking in meaning which they have already heard in the rhythm of speech. For that reason, she always advised beginning with oral exercises (1972b). Periodically, and to be certain that students understand the concept of the phrase, read the first part of a sentence, and ask individual students to complete it orally.

The man carried the groceries . . . .

The rock climber raised himself . . . .

She left her watch . . . .

In his haste to get there, the General drove . . . .

In the dark theater, trying to find the contact lens she had dropped, Alice lost . . . .

The new bridge was built . . . .

Because her Mother wouldn't let her go to the mall alone, she called . . . .

Phrases designating time and location may be used initially to introduce phrasing. Put a list of prepositions (without designating them as prepositions) on the board and ask each student to add to the long list of places a man named Albert might go (*to the lake, over the hill, across the football field*). After this, give students the same kind of elongated sentence, full of phrases, beneath which students may swing their pencils:

With a backpack, full of freeze-dried delicacies, Albert began his ascent of Mount McKinley, by first walking, across gently sloping meadows, then up rock strewn and eroded gullies until he faced the challenge, of the sheer vertical face, of the mountain, which he had to scale, in order to reach the top.

Ansara stated often that one of the most effective aids for a student attempting to read in phrases is the pencil. By swinging a pencil beneath phrases, a student learns to look ahead for the next group of related words (1972b).

Before starting to write, Juliette made herself a ham sandwich, listened to some jazz, combed her hair, washed out a pair of stockings, fed her cat, and watched a horse race on T.V.

Ansara also urged students to buy used textbooks so that they could use pencils freely for phrasing. Paper can be replaced, she insisted, but not the valuable learning years of these students (1966).

SIGNAL WORDS

As work progresses with phrasing, teach students to recognize the often ignored words that signal meaning. These words, that appear so small and insignificant, will not be found in vocabularies with Latin and Greek roots and affixes. They are most often Anglo-Saxon words that signal transition of thought such as: *but, for, because, still, although, however, since,* and *yet*. They are simple words, but charged with the task of signaling negation, contrast, direction, contradiction, comparison, affirmation, relation, prediction, classification, and emphasis. Others qualify, quantify, or express time and location: *more than, most, better, later,* and *deeper.* The concept of one word is understood in relation to its opposite. Words have meaning within the context of other words. Hence, reading is more than decoding. It becomes for students a process of reasoning (Ansara 1972b).

Ask students to review the following sentences and think of the "job" signal words have in a sentence.

Instead of buying a pickup truck, he bought a van.

Since he was leaving for Peru, she decided to buy a ticket for Paris.

Because one student wrote successfully about spiders, the rest of the class wrote essays about beetles, ants, and termites.

I like Joan *but* I like Hildegard more.

I will entrust you with this mission, *if* you follow my instructions.

Although many students are familiar with signal words in speech, they ignore them when reading, and seldom use them in writing. Recognizing signal words is essential for effective phrasing, anticipation of meaning when reading, and written expression. Again, read phrases with signal words to the students and ask them to respond orally.

He wanted to buy the Brooklyn Bridge, *but* . . . .

Without his help, ...

As a result of his decision, ...

During his job as winning coach of the Austin "Eagles," . . . . . .

Fewer than twenty people . . . .

Throughout the night, ...

Frequently, swans swim . . . .

Invariably, her attitude makes me . . . .

Either you make the soup *or* . . . .

Students may simply give one another "signals" to be completed orally.

Several . . . .

Rarely . . . .

Without . . . .

All . . . .

Inasmuch as . . . .

Unfortunately . . . .

Using signal words as transitions for giving directions, put the following words on the blackboard: *first, second, third, next, after, then,* and *finally.* Then ask students to use some of these words in presenting the steps of a recipe, giving directions to some location, or explaining how to make something. Students may also be given a copy of Ansara's list of signal words to use in writing paragraphs or essays.

Qualifying and Quantifying Words

and	when	so that	worse (than)
but	where	besides	better (than)
too	while	sometimes	on the other hand
for	who	nevertheless	provided that
because	what	otherwise	therefore
if	how	in order that	always
no	which	for this reason	yet
not	that	until	indeed
never	all	seldom	to the contrary
so	some	not often	consequently
also	none	infrequently	still
or	few	through	accordingly
either	several	throughout	invariably
neither	many	before	as a result
nor	more	after	finally
as	most	during	indeed
since	less	later	hence

even	fewer (than)	earlier	rarely
though	more (than)	without	although
little more	with	merely	however (than)
much more (than)		inasmuch as	

(Ansara Overhead)

SENTENCE COMBINING

Sentence combining, that is, absorbing phrases and dependent clauses into an independent clause, is more difficult for students with dyslexia because, as many an adolescent mechanic has discovered, taking something apart is much easier than reconstructing it. In this exercise, students construct compound and complex sentences by adding phrases and signal words to simple sentences. Put the following sentence on the blackboard under the heading *simple sentence*.

<u>Simple Sentence</u>

A snake bit a man.

Ask students what they think of this sentence, and they may respond that the sentence is dull, that the reader does not know enough about the incident. Ask students to describe the snake and the man, and tell how the man came to be bitten. Then write the following information on the blackboard.

The snake was a rattlesnake.

The man was a hunter.

The man had been hunting all day.

He was tired.

He was not looking at the ground.

Divide students into teams of two and ask them to consult with one another as they add the information above to the simple sentence. If necessary, allow them to omit words such as *the* and *he*, and to use signal words such as *because* or *since*. When one team comes up with something similar to the following sentence, write it under the heading of *complex sentence*.

<u>Complex Sentence</u>

Because he was tired and not looking at the ground, the hunter was bitten by the rattlesnake.

This exercise should be repeated at least four times or more until you are certain the students understand how to combine sentences. After they have completed this work, ask students to compare and contrast simple sentences and complex sentences. Ask them to write definitions of complex sentences and to share these definitions with other students. If they are able, in their own words, to define *a complex sentence as a simple sentence with phrases and dependent clauses attached to it*, they can record the definition in their notebooks.

At a later time, write two simple sentences (independent clauses) under the heading *simple sentence*.

Simple Sentence

The principal sold his house.

He moved to California.

Ask students to join the two sentences with the conjunction *and*. Under *compound sentence*, write one student's response.

Compound Sentence

The principal sold his house, and he moved to California.

Repeat this exercise.

Simple Sentences

The ceiling was falling down.

No carpenters would fix it.

Ask students to join these independent clauses with the conjunction *but*. One student's work is put on the blackboard under *compound sentence*.

Compound Sentence

The ceiling was falling down, but no carpenters would fix it.

Give three or four more examples and, after discussion, ask for a definition of a compound sentence. If students agree with one student's definition that *a compound sentence is made up of two simple sentences joined by a conjunction*, they may write this definition in their notebooks. It is advisable to review the definitions of *verb, phrase, independent* and *dependent clauses*, and *simple, complex*, and *compound sentences* as often as possible while the students are working with sentence combining.

Finally, to assess students' abilities to combine sentences, allow them to work independently constructing compound or complex sentences from simple sentences. Before they begin, remind them to place commas before the conjunction in compound sentences, after dependent clauses and phrases, after words or phrases in a series, and before and after nonessential words, phrases, and clauses.

The hard rain continued most of the day, and the men would not fight.

Although the greatest battles were over, the war continued in isolated pockets of the country.

Conditions of the peace treaty mandated the removal of all weapons, the construction of small houses for the homeless, and an end to tribal conflicts.

That man, in the fisherman's hat, is my father.

Having a chart hanging in the classroom that illustrates the uses of commas is useful as a reminder for students to punctuate their papers correctly. In the following sentence combining exercises, students use signal words or conjunctions found in the upper right corner.

1. Celia raised Shetland Sheepdogs.   Use *and*.

   Celia raised the dogs in her basement.

   She trained them to become Seeing Eye dogs.

   Celia raised Shetland Sheepdogs in her basement, and trained them to become Seeing Eye dogs.

2. Joshua Speed met Abraham Lincoln.   Use *when*.

   Lincoln moved to Illinois.

   Joshua Speed was a store owner.

   Joshua Speed, a store owner, met Abraham Lincoln when Lincoln moved to Illinois.

3. Mary Highsmith lived alone.   Use *for*.

   She was a ninety-five year old woman.

   She had lived alone for forty years.

   She lived in a big house.

   For forty years, Mary Highsmith, a ninety-five year old woman, lived alone in a big house.

4. The Coharie River flooded.   Use *after* and *and*.

   It rained in July.

   Fifteen inches of rain fell.

   Cars were swept off the road.

5. Mary Highsmith climbed   Use *when* and *although*
   onto her roof.

   She was afflicted with arthritis.

   The flood waters rose fifteen feet.

6. Mary Highsmith was rescued.   Use *although* and *and*

   Her house slid off its foundations.

   It was moving in the tide.

   She was rescued by a helicopter pilot.

7. The river flooded a thousand acres.   Use *since* and *and*.

   There were a thousand acres of soybeans.

   Now only a few treetops could be seen.

   No levees had been built to contain the water.

8. Mary Highsmith moved into a condominium.   Use *and*.

   She moved after the flood.

   The condominium is for "swinging singles."

   Now she enjoys raising azaleas on her rooftop garden.

Although students may soon feel confident reading phrases and anticipating meaning, they will not feel truly proficient until they are able to spell and write phrases and signal words. Therefore, after students have read a list of simple phrases, such as *by the river*, begin dictating some of the same phrases. Have students repeat a phrase, write it, and say it again. However, before dictating phrases, have students learn familiar signal words (See previous lesson.), such as *before, after, when, since, although, for, during, over, because, however,* and *while*. Many signal words, such as *although*, are nonphonetic, and a student may have to trace over the word and name the letters several times. When students can spell these words correctly, dictate phrases that begin with the signal words students have learned. Depending on the severity of a student's disability, you may or may not choose to display the phrase while dictating it. Students repeat the phrase, write it, then say it again. The following list of phrases are for dictation.

During the night	After too many rides
Over the rainbow	After they left
Although it is raining	Since we are leaving
Before she goes	Under the train
While he slept	With heavy feet
Without an umbrella	Above ground
Before leaving	Through the looking glass
When he returns	Because I know
Since he left	Before you go
Later that night	Early in the morning
Until then	While buying shoes
Because of you	When we jog
For all that	Either of you
Between the acts	Over the fence
While cooking	Among friends
Although he knew	Down in the grass
While he was working	Between the two storms
Under the log	By the fire
With someone	During the night
While breathing	Up on the hill

After a week, dictate some of the same phrases again. The same words can be used also in paragraph or essay writing. When students are confident in their ability to recognize and to use phrases and signal words, they will begin to achieve a more rapid understanding of an author's intent, and academic success will become a real possibility.

Exercise for Phrasing and Signal Words

Complete the following:

1. **Aboard** the old ship, _____
2. **Above** the storm, _____
3. **According** to the radio report, _____
4. **Across** the muddy water, _____
5. **After** the tornado hit Dallas, _____
6. **Against** the heavy wind, _____
7. **Along** the spacious boulevard, _____
8. **Among** his old friends, _____
9. **Around** the edge of the yard, _____
10. **At** the corner of Ninth and Main, _____
11. **Because** she was sick, _____
12. **Before** the circus began, _____
13. **Behind** the shady brick building, _____
14. **Below** the high sand dunes, _____
15. **Beneath** the floorboards, _____
16. **Beside** the decaying log, _____
17. **Between** his aunt and uncle _____
18. **By** the pink lawn chairs, _____
19. **Despite** many interruptions, _____
20. **During** her job as a waitress, _____
21. **For** all he cared, _____
22. **From** the heart of the city, _____
23. **Inside** the crowded newsroom, _____
24. **Into** the new house, _____
25. **Off** the back porch, _____
26. **On account of** her interest in butterflies, _____
27. **Outside** the city, _____
28. **Over** the blue mountains, _____
29. **Past** the Black Hills, _____
30. **Through** their mutual efforts, _____
31. **Throughout** the long night, _____

32. **To** the ends of the earth, _____

33. **Underneath** the basement floor, _____

34. **Up** the avenue of Live Oak trees, _____

35. **Either** you plan the trip or _____

36. **Although** he seemed undefeatable, _____

37. **As soon as** you return, _____

38. **Because** the leading actor was ill, _____

39. **However** much you protest, _____

40. **Even** if you write a great novel, _____

41. **If** you do succeed in becoming president, _____

42. **Provided** the chorus arrives on time, _____

43. **When** the first "Star Trek" series appeared on television, _____

44. **Unless** they release the hostages soon, _____

45. **When** all the nations in the world confer, _____

46. **Whenever** the birds begin to fly South, _____

47. **Wherever** the leaves fall, _____

48. **While** you may want to go to college, _____

Time: Six Weeks or Longer

PLANNING SUGGESTIONS

I. Objectives: Students will understand the meanings of *phrase, sentence, dependent clause, complex* and *compound sentences*. Their reading will become more fluent as they are able to isolate phrases with their pencils and begin to anticipate meaning through an awareness of signal words. Students will also be able to build complex and compound sentences through sentence-combining exercises. In addition, they will know how to use the library and be able to find all sources of information there.

II. Materials: Student notebooks, lists of phrases, signal words,and sentence-combining activities, and copies of the Dewey Decimal System.

III. Procedures:

A. Students continue to work on syllabication, vocabulary, and spelling.

B. Ask students to complete phrases that you give them orally (*High in the nebulous clouds* . . .). Give individual students phrases on slips of paper and ask them to make a sentence of these on the blackboard. Again on the blackboard or overhead, make two columns for *sentence* and *other* and begin putting examples under each heading (*He is buying a car* and *Buying a car*). Students compare these examples and after many more examples may conclude that a sentence has a verb. Make a list of verbs in the sentences, and try to elicit a definition. If someone says "action word," then you can obtain a definition of a sentence as needing a verb and expressing a complete thought.

C. Introduce the concept of dependent clauses with examples and nonexamples until students come up with the definition. Put phrases designating time and location on the blackboard, and have students make an elongated sentence out of them (*Late in the afternoon, near a stream* . . .). At this point, students should begin reading in textbooks or other available books, lightly looping the pencil under phrases. Also begin dictation of phrases using the S.O.S. technique.

D. At this point introduce signal words, those words that signal transition of thought, such as *but, however, still, since, yet, throughout* and perform the important function of signaling meaning. Ask students to complete sentences that begin with words such as *Nevertheless, Either, Invariably,* and *Finally* orally and then give them similar written work.

E. Introduce complex and compound sentences by providing examples and nonexamples of each, and by beginning with a simple sentence and having students add dependent clauses and phrases to make it a complex sentence. To demonstrate the concept of *compound sentences*, write two simple sentences and have students join them with *and* or *but*.

F. Finally, introduce students to sentence combining by giving them dependent clauses and phrases to add to a simple sentence. Proceed slowly with this exercise because many students may find it difficult.

G. When instructing students on Library use (see page 175), pass out copies of the Dewey Decimal System in your classroom. Explain how books are catalogued under particular call numbers and ask students where one would find books on American history, art, philosophy, religion, and woodworking. Then take students to the library and show them the reference section with encyclopedias, almanacs, and dictionaries. Show them how biographies and fiction are catalogued, and where the newspapers and magazines are located. Explain more about the resources to be found on the Internet, and follow up with individual library assignments.

IV. Evaluation: Have students use their list of signal words to write a long paragraph using at least twelve words from the list. Have them isolate and write twenty phrases that they find in a book. Give the students a sheet with information they must find in the library and take them there.

Chapter 9

Comprehension:
Making Connections

When students with dyslexia begin reading more fluently and anticipating thought, they will find doors to a body of knowledge and experience begin to open for them. They may now be reading fiction for pleasure, learning to empathize with the conflicts of the main characters, reading biographies or autobiographies, and newspapers and magazines. As students enrich their vocabularies, they are better able to understand and to make inferences about what they are reading. With this new confidence, students begin to reconnect with themselves, peers, families, and with the learning process itself. However, as Alice Ansara (1966) pointed out, like other students with reading difficulties, students with dyslexia may still have problems finding and interpreting an author's intent.

In her discussion of the reasons for reading, Ansara noted that people read for relaxation, intellectual and emotional needs, particular information, knowledge, and to satisfy curiosity. Each kind of reading involves a specific interpretive skill. For instance, the casual reading of mystery or romance novels does not demand the serious emotional or intellectual consideration or attention to language that the reading of "classical" literature requires. Reading essays, editorials, textbooks, or other nonfiction requires critical discernment and the weighing of facts and ideas. In researching information for term papers, students must be able to scan for information, skimming over unnecessary words and details to find main ideas (Ansara 1966). Unfortunately, it is hard to determine how well students with dyslexia interpret an author's intent because they often expend much time and energy trying to locate statements of purpose in paragraphs and essays.

Many students with dyslexia have difficulty with part-to-whole relationships. This is demonstrated in geography class, for instance, when a student cannot easily perceive how a county is a unit within the larger units of state, nation, and global community. In English class, a student may be unable to separate main from subordinate ideas in an outline, or cannot grasp the concept of "narrowing" a topic. As previously mentioned, this part-to-whole confusion is also evident when a student attempts to sort through supporting statements to find a main idea in nonfiction writing. Whatever the cause, the problem must be addressed because it is vital that students understand an author's purpose for writing, as well as be able to identify main ideas for essays in high school and college.

To help students become more discerning in locating main ideas, read aloud from paragraphs and essays in textbooks, and from students' own writings. Question students about the author's intentions. Urge students to read aloud and to ask questions also.

> I went into the woods because I wished to live deliberately, to front only the essential facts of life, and see if I could not learn what it had to teach, and not, when I came to die, discover that I had not lived. I did not wish to live what was not life, living is so dear. . . .
>
> (Thoreau from *Walden*)

Why did Thoreau go into the woods to live? How did he want to live? What did he want to learn? What are the "essential facts of life"? Can anyone imagine going into the woods to live "deliberately"? What would you think if a friend decided to live like Thoreau? It is very important that students, themselves, learn to ask relevant questions. (Students with dyslexia often are reluctant to ask questions and seldom give complete oral or written responses.)

Having students write summaries of what they have read also enhances their ability to isolate main ideas. *A summary is a brief form of a longer piece of fiction or nonfiction.* When summarizing fiction, a writer should identify main characters and events, including setting and plot progression. In nonfiction, a writer should include a statement about the main idea, list supportive details, and include important names, dates, and places, in proper order. When writing summaries of both fiction and non-fiction, a writer is advised to use his or her own words as succinctly as possible (Haley-James and Stewig 1993).

Many secondary teachers assume that most students have the prerequisite skills for writing summaries and paragraphs. After reading the half-answered, incoherent, and fragmented responses to essay questions, teachers begin to realize that a number of students cannot write complete sentences, formulate opinions, or support them adequately. To conclude, however, as some teachers do, that these students are incapable of writing logical and complete answers only reinforces a pattern of negativity and failure.

If you assess what students know about writing skills, you may find that there are still students who do not know what a sentence is. On finding this, take time to review a sentence as a unit of thought and discuss the kinds of sentences: statement (declarative), question (interrogative), command (imperative), and that which expresses strong feeling and ends with an exclamation mark (exclamatory).

During the fire, a man did call for help.

Did a man call for help?

Call for help.

I need help!

By insisting that students answer questions completely, and by giving them assignments, such as telling brief stories (humorous tall tales) with enough details to make them convincing, you will discover that students soon become more confident with oral presentations, and, as a result, with written work. In addition, having a student describe how to make something—a chair, a dress, a hat, a speech, or a good impression—and to convince others to make it is an effective way of introducing paragraphs.

Alice Ansara thought that too often teachers convince students that a main idea or topic sentence is to be found in the first sentence of a paragraph (1966). In fact, the main idea may be at the beginning, middle, or end of a paragraph, as can be seen in the following three paragraphs.

The society of the African wild dog is founded on the pack. Unlike a lion pride or a hyena clan, the wild dog pack stays together no matter what animal they are hunting. The wild dogs are nomads and travel together in packs of five to thirty members, always moving together to new areas, sometimes twenty-five miles away (Marler 1972).

In an essay,"Why Do We Read Fiction?"Robert Penn Warren states that we read fiction because we enjoy reading it. Fiction reflects life and stimulates our interest in life. But the particular interest of the reader of fiction is in the way individuals strive to overcome conflict and to move towards an appropriate resolution. When we become absorbed in a story, we experience a surge of the intense vitality usually felt during play or adventure, and delight in an opportunity to release our emotions, as threatening problems are being solved (Warren 1968).

Small towns in the Great Plains states are declining rapidly. Young people are moving to the cities, leaving an aging population behind. In 1990, Kansas had more "frontier land," that is, fewer than six people per square mile than it did a century ago. Although thousands of acres have been acquired for prairie grass and bison in order to promote tourism, the question of small town decline is still a problem. One answer to this dilemma is the belief that through technology, such as the Internet, communities can share resources, and individuals can start businesses which may sustain the population in these isolated prairie towns (Cohen 1998).

The main idea may be implied, not stated at all:

On Thursday at 8:00 A.M., near Baton Rouge, a barge loaded with toxic chemicals sank in the Mississippi River. Two miles away, school children got off the yellow buses parked as usual in front of Wilson Elementary School. Vendors, drinking coffee and chatting among themselves, set up vegetable stalls at the Farmers Market, and a silvery stream of cars continued over the Mississippi Bridge and into the city.

Writing descriptive paragraphs is a useful exercise in paragraph writing. Students can describe a scene in nature, a house, person, or a piece of fruit. Lists of adjectives can be given to the students to enrich their vocabularies and stimulate their writing. Students still must state an opinion or a reason for choosing to describe a friend, an abandoned house, or a spider building a web. They must provide supporting details and examples; and they must be aware of order, of moving from the general to the specific or vice versa. For example, students may first describe the facade of an abandoned house, the general plan of the interior, and then the furniture in each room. Writing descriptive paragraphs will make students more conscious of the sights, sounds, smells, tastes, and textures of their environment. If students appear uncertain about choosing topics, provide them with photographs, postcards, paintings, or objects they may choose to describe.

After they have been reading and writing paragraphs on a daily basis, students can begin the process of writing their own short essays. By going through the discipline of selecting a topic, narrowing a topic, and writing a topic sentence, students will inevitably become more adept at recognizing the purpose of another author. Before beginning this process, however, give students the following terms to find in the dictionary to discuss in class and to record in their notebooks: *essay, fact, opinion, bias, propaganda, persuasion, description, identify, define, describe, compare,* and *contrast.*

Before beginning their own short essays, students ordinarily go through an important brainstorming session to come up with their own topics. For this particular exercise, allow five students to write general topics on the blackboard:

sports   pets   movies   hobbies   books

Explain that volumes could be written about these general topics, but, for a short essay, students must narrow the topic to a particular sport, pet, movie, hobby, or book.

football   Golden Retrievers   *Gone with the Wind*
stamp collecting   The Hobbit

Because these topics are still too broad for short essays, urge students to narrow them further. These phrases illustrate the result:

The only winning football game.

Golden Retrievers, friendly guard dogs.

Greedy Scarlett O'Hara.

Preserving stamps for the future.

No women characters in *The Hobbit.*

Before students write topic sentences, which may be opinions, assess the students' abilities by giving them statements like the following to see if they can distinguish facts from opinions.

Fifty inches of rain fell on Las Vegas during the Winter of 1997.

This was one of the worst winters I have ever known.

World War II began in 1939.

Martin Luther King believed in nonviolence.

It's going to rain tomorrow.

If students understand the meaning of *opinion*, they can begin writing topic sentences for their essays. Because this is such a difficult task, give them extra time so they do not feel stressed.

> The Blue Eagles finally showed their superiority by beating the Falcons after an unbelievable touchdown by Bob Dunn.

> Because we were robbed twice, I think Golden Retrievers are too friendly to be good guard dogs.

> Her relationships make it clear that Scarlett O'Hara cared only for herself, her home, and money.

> Placing sheets of stamps between plastic is the best way of preserving them.

> For women readers of The Hobbit, finding no adventuring female Hobbits in the book is a big disappointment.

The process of narrowing topics (of making them specific) and writing topic sentences should continue each day before students begin reading paragraphs or writing essays. The importance of these skills cannot be ignored. Many an essay writer in college has discovered about twenty pages too late, that the idea he or she was developing was not the real intent at all. More work may be necessary to help students understand what it means to form and express opinions. A few students inevitably write statements of fact, but when they begin to realize how difficult it is to write more about such statements, they abandon them and write opinions.

Forming teams for debates may be useful. Students generate rules for the debate, with polite behavior stressed, and each student chooses to be *pro* or *con* in relation to a given topic. Each debater supports his or her opinion with three or four examples, facts, illustrations, or other information. Again, the importance of having students understand terms such as *opinion, bias,* and *propaganda* will be of value when, as adult citizens, they begin to evaluate political rhetoric. When the debate is concluded, have students brainstorm for topics for their essays. They may choose one from their lists, narrow it, and write topic sentences. Then they develop outlines. As students go through a number of ideas to be used in their papers, it will be clear that some of these are main ideas and others, subordinate ideas. Outlines are very useful for clarifying thoughts and for covering the essential points of an essay question on a test.

No Women in *The Hobbit*

A. Feeling of exclusion

    1. No women among the heroes

    2. No women among the wicked

B. Lack of role models

    1. Need for women adventurers

    2. Need for women warriors

As the student writes, he or she must also remember to use transition words and phrases to signal introductions, to make additions, or show relationships: *for example, for instance, in addition (to), also, besides, furthermore, because, therefore, similarly, yet, however, nevertheless, moreover,* and *though.*

Writing an essay of comparison and contrast is a formidable task for many students with dyslexia. Have them begin by putting the words *like* and *unlike* on the blackboard and let them find ways in which two people, objects, or ideas are alike and ways in which they are different. Just as many students will not complete the second part in a two-part question, or neglect to describe in an identify and describe question, when asked to compare and contrast, they will frequently compare and forget to contrast or vice versa. When writing a comparison and contrast paragraph or essay, remind students to:

Liken and contrast two persons, events, ideas, objects, or opinions;

Define the likenesses and differences of each item clearly;

Use examples, details, facts, or figures to support statements;

Describe all the characteristics of one person or thing before describing the characteristics of another person or thing; or

Make a point-by-point comparison of two items.

Reading and writing essays will help the adolescent with dyslexia discover an author's intent, and this skill, with vocabulary building, will inevitably increase comprehension. Alice

Ansara (1978) thought that the overall goal for students with dyslexia, and for all students, should be "reading as a process of reasoning." In a letter to Richard McKay (1977), Ansara stated that reading provides food for the intellect, and those deprived of this ability suffer lifelong deprivation. Without the proper training from teachers or language therapists, many students with reading problems will never achieve their learning potential.

To demonstrate the interlocking skills that are the underpinnings of the reading process, Ansara composed a chart of the "Building Blocks" of reading (1966). For those adolescents with dyslexia, who have begun step-by-step and successfully mastered the skills necessary for reading comprehension, Ansara would have quoted Jose Marti, the Cuban poet, who wrote, "To know how to read is to know how to walk."

SOME READING AND STUDY SKILLS FOR ADOLESCENTS THAT ARE PREREQUISITES FOR A SUCCESSFUL SCHOOL PERFORMANCE

There are many skills essential for successful school performance by the time a child enters the junior high school and encounters schedules and curricula modeled on the senior high school. These skills must not only be learned but practiced in order to be mastered. Some of the reading and study skills are given below to serve you as a checklist.

1. Syllabication of unfamiliar words.

2. Structural analysis of unfamiliar words.

3. Vocabulary acquisition through association of roots and affixes.

4. Recognition and understanding of words that signal transition of thought.

5. Recognition and understanding of words that qualify, i.e., words that express time, space, quantity, or degree.

6. Recognition and understanding of phrases as thought units that not only carry their own meanings but signal meanings to come.

7. Recognition and understanding of relationships within complex sentences and ability to deal with subordination and coordination.

8. Recognition and understanding of various forms of organization in paragraph construction.

9. Recognition and understanding of a central theme in connected paragraphs.

10. Ability to preview, survey, skim, and scan for various purposes, or prior to a fuller reading.

11. Recognition of clues to content in study materials: pictures, graphs, tables, bold type, italics, or headings.

12. Ability to outline as a means of identifying important concepts and their supporting ideas and details.

13. Ability to place new information within a frame of familiar reference and be able to relate the two for heightened awareness and understanding.

14. Ability to distinguish between direct statements and implied meanings.

15. Ability to arrive at logical conclusions based upon the material read.

16. Ability to understand the format of a textbook and to use that format to good advantage.

17. Ability to use various reference materials: dictionary, encyclopedias, index, card catalogue, or [computer].

18. Ability to vary rate of reading according to purpose.

19. Ability to read, formulate [one's] own thoughts in relation to new information, and to summarize it.

20. A developing ability to be selective in choice of reading.

Alice Ansara

Building Blocks of Reading

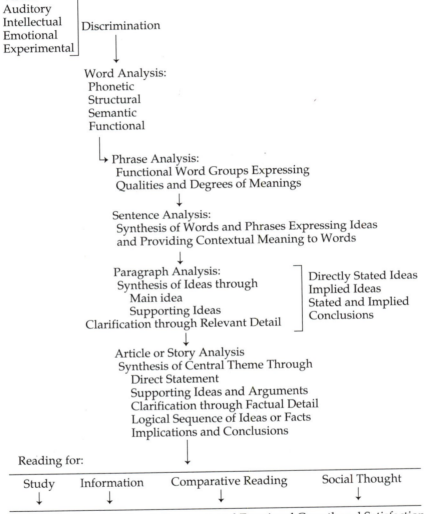

Visual
Auditory
Intellectual — Discrimination
Emotional
Experimental

Word Analysis:
Phonetic
Structural
Semantic
Functional

Phrase Analysis:
Functional Word Groups Expressing
Qualities and Degrees of Meanings

Sentence Analysis:
Synthesis of Words and Phrases Expressing Ideas
and Providing Contextual Meaning to Words

Paragraph Analysis: Directly Stated Ideas
Synthesis of Ideas through   Implied Ideas
Main idea   Stated and Implied
Supporting Ideas   Conclusions
Clarification through Relevant Detail

Article or Story Analysis
Synthesis of Central Theme Through
Direct Statement
Supporting Ideas and Arguments
Clarification through Factual Detail
Logical Sequence of Ideas or Facts
Implications and Conclusions

Reading for:

Study	Information	Comparative Reading	Social Thought

Intellectual, Social, Cultural, Economic and Emotional Growth and Satisfaction

(Ansara 1966)

Time: Two Months

PLANNING SUGGESTIONS

I. Objectives: Students will understand the various reasons people read. They will also be able to write complete sentences, paragraphs, essays that compare and contrast, describe, and state a position. They will know how to choose a topic, narrow it, write a topic sentence, an outline, and a short research paper.

II. Materials: Student notebooks, paper, pens, note cards, models of sentences, paragraphs, essays, outlines, and a research paper.

III. Procedures:

A. Continue to work on syllabication, vocabulary, spelling, and phrasing.

B. Ask students why people read. Urge them to remember relatives who did enjoy reading and the kinds of material they read. List sources of reading material—labels, signs, directions, job applications, driver's manual, magazines, newspapers, romance novels, biographies, travel and adventure books, and what is called "great literature." Have students write about a culture (imaginative or real) in which no one reads.

C. While still discussing the purpose of reading, give students models of sentences, paragraphs, essays, an outline, and research a paper for reading, discussion, and study.

D. Begin a daily practice of narrowing or limiting general topics (*sports* to *football* to *a famous linebacker*). Discuss the merits of writing that is specific rather than general. Have students give general topics to other students for narrowing. reverse the process and give specifics and have students find the general categories for specifics (*Lassie* to *collie* to *herding dogs* to *mammals* to *ani-*

mals). Let students decide, from word examples, which type of thinking process—deductive or inductive thinking—they are using when they narrow or broaden a topic.

E. Have students choose topics and begin narrowing them. When you are certain students understand this process, have them write topic sentences, statements expressing opinions. Discuss where topic sentences are placed in a paragraph, and how opinions must be supported by examples, facts, or observations. Have students write summaries of essays that include the topic sentences. Help students create transitions between paragraphs.

F. Have students write short essays that compare and contrast, that state a position, or that describe a person or situation.

G. Before students begin a research paper, teach them how to make outlines, to prioritize topics and subtopics, and to include facts and examples. Have them write an outline prioritizing the various facts of a particular concern.

H. When students are ready to begin work on their research paper, help them choose a topic that interests them, find source material in the library, narrow the topic, write a statement of purpose, and make an outline. In addition, explain the use of note cards, and bibliography. Help students in every stage of research and writing, and especially in documenting their sources.

IV. Evaluation: Teacher will assess essays, outlines, and research papers. Students will also evaluate their own work.

Chapter 10

Study Skills

For students to succeed in secondary school and later, in college, they must have the skills and motivation to do independent work. Yet, for many reasons, whether they be poverty, a home environment that is not conducive to study, non-supportive parents, responsibility for younger children, or peers who denigrate education, many adolescents are unable to complete the homework required for their courses. Even for motivated students, poor nutrition and a lack of three meals a day can make nourishment a goal of such immediacy that homework and plans for the future may seem remote and unrealistic (Ansara 1966). When students also have reading difficulties, the problem is compounded.

Teachers are familiar with those students who struggle to find words in the dictionary, are barely able to read through the introduction of a textbook, and do not understand the directions on a test; but there is also another, less obvious problem—that of teacher perception and expectation. Alice Ansara (1966) observed that reading teachers often perceive students with specific language disabilities as being unable to "function intellectually on a par with those who have been in the upper stream of the educational process." Teachers who see "bundles of deficits" rather than multi-faceted human beings, inevitably lower their expectations and begin to think in terms of methods, and not of thought and language. Consequently, they may neglect to teach the vital study skills that would enable these students to become independent learners. In addition, adolescents affected by teacher perceptions and expectations, may not be motivated to try to do better work because they perceive themselves to be "disabled" by their language problems. These students may come to class without notebooks, pencils, pens, or textbooks—characteristics of students who have given up, who have no expectations beyond daily exigencies, and who may choose, now that they are not invested in learning, to become class clowns, to become even more disruptive, or to drop out of school altogether. (Although seemingly insignificant, having students bring their "tools" to class is of major importance, because indifferent students take the same attitude to their work place after high school.) If these same students had been recognized and applauded in the past for talents in drawing, musical ability, repairing cars, growing plants, acting, dancing, leadership, original thoughts, or compassion in relating to other students, they might have begun to believe they could also learn to read and write with more proficiency. The recently developed concept of multiple intelligences, that is, of linguistic, logical-mathematical, spatial, bodily-kinesthetic, musical, interpersonal, and intrapersonal intelligences, is an effort to broaden the narrow definition of intelligence traditionally assigned to linguistic or mathematical capabilities (Armstrong 1994).

Knowing each student's strengths enables teachers to design a variety of assignments that accommodate particular talents. A student who reads poorly, is less likely to be ridiculed if other students are aware that he or she is a fine guitar player. In an essay comparing the similarities and differences of gifted and dyslexic students, Ansara wrote of the incredible variation among children in any classroom—in their patterns of thinking, language abilities, energy and self-esteem, social relations, arts, and mechanics—and she concluded by stating that if we are aware of these variations, we will also know that "there are no exceptional children, only different children, each with certain needs" (1979).

For students with or without dyslexia, academic success in high school is largely dependent on self-esteem, reading and written language ability, and possessing crucial study skills. Learning to keep a notebook in order, to write down homework assignments, and to become responsible for completing assignments should be regarded as vital preconditioning for that success. But confident and independent learners are those who also know strategies for surveying texts, studying, taking notes and tests, making outlines, and using a dictionary and the library.

SURVEYING TEXTBOOKS

Begin the school year by teaching students how to survey textbooks. This is one of the first skills an adolescent with dyslexia must acquire. When textbooks are assigned, many students receive them with feelings of dread and frustration. Past experience is of words not understood and chapters never completed because of word-by-word reading habits. Halting readers, whose way of coping with the "burden" of textbooks is mainly one of avoidance, experience no sense of ownership, of being able to anticipate information that will soon be taught. They forget to bring texts to class or leave them at home. Occasionally, motivated students and parents will ask for second texts to keep at home because of these problems.

To alleviate apprehension and frustration, you, as the teacher, should become familiar with the texts your students are using in order to analyze format, style, and vocabulary. Introduce students to author, title, date of publication, publisher, preface or foreword, table of contents, glossary of special terms, appendix, and index. The *preface* or *foreword* may give an indication of the purpose of the book and how it should be used. The *table of contents* often represents an outline of the book, and should be read carefully because it may contain the main topics and subtopics in the book. The *glossary* is an alphabetical list of special terms. The *appendix* (if there is one) should be noted as a place for the clarification of certain material in the text; and the *index* is an alphabetical list of people and subjects to be found on designated pages in the text (Ansara 1966; 1972b).

Before beginning a chapter analysis, give students an information-finding assignment in their textbooks concerning the main topic of the book, identifications in the index, a chapter on a special topic, the author's purpose in writing the book, the definition of a particular term, and specific information in the appendix. Students then search for the meanings of *preface, table of contents, appendix, glossary,* and *index* in the dictionary, write the definitions, and file them in the vocabulary section of their notebooks.

When the text has been completely surveyed, begin chapter study. If there is an introduction or a summary at the end of the chapter, read these first so that students understand briefly what the chapter is about. Reading the questions at the end of a chapter is also a good way to begin. By becoming familiar with the questions, a student will more quickly understand the meaning of the topics in bold print and sentences in italics throughout the chapter. The student can also examine pictures, graphs, and illustrations before beginning to read the text. By obtaining information this way with very little reading, the student can anticipate assignments in the textbook, in lectures and facilitate note-taking (Ansara 1972b). An example of an information-finding assignment is given below.

Find the following information in your textbook:

1. Title _____
2. Author _____
3. Publication Date _____
4. Publishing Company _____
5. Place of Publication _____

In what section of the book is the following information?

6. The title of a chapter in the book _____
7. Special vocabulary terms _____
8. More references about a person mentioned in the text
   _____
9. The author(s) purpose in writing the text _____
10. A list of writings used by the author on the same subject _____

Does each chapter have

11. An introduction? _____
12. Questions and/or a summary at the end? _____
13. Photographs, drawings, and/or graphs? _____
14. Subtopics in bold print? (Name one) _____
15. Vocabulary words in italics? (Name one) _____

STRATEGIES FOR STUDY

Since reading has been such a formidable obstacle for students with dyslexia, many of them have not developed methods for studying that will enable them to cope with their course work. Often students who listen well and have good memories rely upon the lectures they hear in class, but the information gathered from lectures and class discussions will not compensate for not having read the text.

One basic study approach recommended by Alice Ansara is the "SQ3R" technique developed by Francis P. Robinson. The first step of this approach is to *survey* the chapter to be studied. After reading the summary, questions, and vocabulary at the end in order to anticipate key ideas, events, noteworthy persons, and other important information, students read the introduction and skim through the chapter looking at pictures, graphs, and maps. After reading topics and subtopics in bold print, they turn statements into *questions*. For example, the heading, "The War of 1812" becomes a question: "What was the War of 1812?" By turning a statement into a question, students are more prepared to absorb the information that answers the questions. The longer students spend questioning, the more likely it is that they will remember the material.

After surveying the chapter, turning statements into questions, and noting words in bold print and italics, students *read* carefully, considering whether the author's main ideas have merit and whether the ideas are reasonably supported by facts and examples. Questioning should continue as students read the text closely. Answers can be underlined, and notes written in the margin. (Unfortunately, most students are not able to buy their texts and are prohibited from making marks in books. Occasionally, special educators are given a certain number of texts that they can highlight and continue to use for their students.) By summarizing an author's thoughts, students make them their own. Also, by summarizing or highlighting important ideas, students are better able to review main ideas without having to sift through details (Ansara 1966).

Occasionally, students should pause and see if they can *recite* or summarize what they have read. This step is very important because by reciting aloud or writing a short summary of what has been read, students are able to grasp more fully the author's intent. In addition, if students reflect, and try to link what they have learned to their own experiences, creative thinking starts to take place (Millman and Pauk 1969).

Finally, and this, too, is an important step, students should *review* often, skimming over the chapters, reading introductions, summaries, and main ideas. They should also review classnotes daily, rewriting them, if necessary, in order to clarify the material. By developing this habit of systematic review, students can avoid the frustration and panic of last minute "cramming," assured that when they are tested, they will know what they need to know.

Demonstrate the SQ3R technique when all students have the same reading assignment for a particular course. After a demonstration and discussion, ask students to describe this technique, and to consider how it could improve their study habits.

TAKING NOTES

Learning how to take notes is an essential skill for any student who wants to become an independent learner. Frequently, students with language difficulties borrow notes from classmates or teachers, or try to pass a class without taking any notes, because they tend to write slowly and have spelling problems. Although some students bring tape recorders to class, they will probably have to transcribe main ideas for study when listening to the tapes once; otherwise it would take hours to review all the tapes for a test. This is, in fact, the task of notetakers—to recognize main ideas and to transcribe them briefly and clearly.

To prepare students for notetaking, read newspaper articles aloud and ask students to find the *who, what, when, where, why* and *how* information. Explain that different academic classes require different kinds of information. In English class, when studying literature, students may need to know information about the setting, mood, plot, characters, climax, and resolution. In history, students may need to know major characters, dates, events, and results. In math, students may need to record algorithms, models of graphs, concepts, and formulas for calculation. In science, students may need to record names of major scientists, explain their ideas or the results of lab studies, or identify the properties of particular elements.

Besides knowing key information to record in different classes, students must also know how to abbreviate and omit unnecessary words when notetaking. Again, approach this task orally, giving students main ideas, which, like newspaper headings, need to be shortened.

> There was an explosion in the science lab at Central High School on Monday when a student mistakenly mixed the wrong compounds. No students in the lab were injured.

> *Explosion in science lab at central high, but no injuries.*

City Council members unanimously approved one million dollars for paving streets in the city.

> *Council members approve one million for street paving.*

Writing summaries while reading assignments in texts is an excellent way for students to begin notetaking. If, for example, students are reading a chapter for history on World War II, they may choose to write summaries, that is, brief accounts about World War II in their own words.

Writing *summaries* is also excellent practice for reluctant writers. Writers should avoid copying statements from the text, however, because they will not understand what they have learned. Students should write quickly, and check their spelling later. The summary should be written in complete statements.

> World War II began after the Germans invaded Poland in 1939, and Britain and France declared war on Germany.

Students with dyslexia need practice in writing complete sentences, but in order to take notes in class, they must also learn to make abbreviated notes and develop a system of shorthand. All unnecessary words should be deleted.

> World War II began in 1939 when Ger. invaded Pol. & Brit., & Fr. declared war on Ger.

Summarizing the text will give students a lucid set of notes, an increased understanding of what must be learned, and practice finding main ideas and transcribing them in their own words (Armstrong and Lampe 1983).

Another useful way of taking notes from a text is by outlining a chapter. This, too, is a valuable experience because students must find and arrange the main topic, subtopics, and supporting details in a logical order (see Outlining, p. 171).

I. Causes of World War II

A. Economic depression in Germany.

B. German aggression.

Students, who do not want to write summaries or outlines, may develop charts or maps on which to assemble information. Using colored pens or pencils, they can make charts on which to file information.

World War II

Dates	Causes	Events	Major Characters	Consequences
1939	German aggression	Invasion of Poland	Hitler, Churchill	Britain & Fr. declare war

(Jensen 1982)

This same chart can also be used for taking notes in class. Students, however, may need to have more space for additional information.

A student who does not like the rigidity of a chart, may choose to make a "map" instead. Again, the student may use colors to clarify the map.

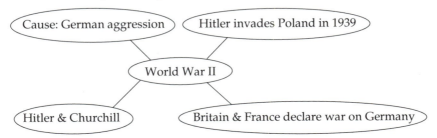

Depending on individual learning styles, students will choose one of the notetaking techniques above or perhaps another more original one. No matter which techniques students choose, however, they must be able to isolate key words, and they must learn to listen well. In some courses, 50% to 80% of the course material is given orally (Armstrong and Lampe 1983). Listening takes practice and discipline. In order to listen well, students should avoid distractions by having paper, pens, and/or pencils organized and on their desks. They should think about the teacher's message, ask questions when they do not understand, pay close attention, focus on key ideas, and try to anticipate what the teacher is going to say next.

For students who have no particular notetaking techniques, but who usually write down whatever they think is important, the following strategy may be helpful. Students make a vertical line down the center of their paper. On the right side they take notes, and on the left side they summarize the notes later, after class. After writing their summaries, and without looking at notes, students recite what they remember, trying to link what they have learned to something in their own experience. In a week, they review both notes and summaries (Millman and Pauk 1962).

The ability to discern which ideas have greater importance than others takes time, motivation, and experience. As students with dyslexia learn to concentrate, to listen, to grasp main ideas, and to choose the right format for recording these ideas, they will develop the confidence to become independent learners.

TAKING TESTS

Before taking tests, students should review notes taken in class, the important readings from the text, and, rather than being overwhelmed by negative feelings, calmly recite what they know. After enough sleep, students should come to class with pencils, pens, paper or whatever else is required. Before administering a test, however, you, as the teacher, should instruct students in the strategies that will help them become more proficient test takers:

1. Always look over the entire test before answering any questions.

2. If there are two essay questions at the end, do not linger over objective test items such as true-false, matching, or multiple choice. Your first response to a multiple choice question is likely to be the correct one.

   In true-false questions, be wary of qualifying words such as *usually* or *rarely*. The answers must be true or false without exceptions.

3. Work carefully, but as quickly as possible, trying to answer all questions. If you are unable to answer a question, mark it lightly with a pencil, and return to it after finishing the rest of the test.

4. Read instructions and questions carefully. Be sure not to underline if asked to circle an answer.

5. Try not to misread words. If there are directions or words that you do not understand, ask the examiner for clarification. If you do not understand the meanings of *define, describe, explain, identify,* and *compare* and *contrast,* ask the teacher for definitions of these terms..

   Define means to state the exact meaning of a word.

   Describe means to make an impression with words. (For example, if a student were to describe a character in literature, he or she might tell how the person looked, talked and acted).

   Explain means to offer reasons for an event, or to make something understood.

Identify means defining who a person is or what a person does, or stating the definite classification of an object or idea.

Compare means to find similarities.

Contrast means to find differences.

6. In two-part test items such as <u>compare and contrast</u> or <u>identify and describe</u>, do not neglect to answer the second part of the question, and thereby receive only half credit for a partially correct answer.

7. Before answering essay questions, jot down ideas about each one on scrap paper or in the margin of the test. Reread the question and make a small outline of the main points before beginning. For example, if asked to explain the causes of World War I, think about the question and then make a small outline.

Causes of WWI

    A. Military alliances

    B. Expansionism

These mini-outlines will help you remember the main ideas in the answer. Always begin by turning a question into a statement, and by answering in complete sentences (Millman and Pauk 1969).

The causes of World War I were military alliances and expansionism.

The writer will also support this statement by discussing military alliances and European expansionism.

8. Finally, glance over the test before giving it to the teacher. Be sure you have read the questions correctly and have responded to all questions, accurately.

PRACTICE TEST

Answer **True** or **False**.

1. _____ Before beginning, I have read through the entire test.

2. _____ Native Americans may have lived in this country before Europeans settled here.

3. _____ Shakespeare was a famous World War II pilot.

4. _____ Usually, teachers give good rather than bad grades.

5. _____ Dictionaries are always easy to read.

Circle the letter of the correct answer.

6. George Washington lived here in his old age.

   a. Delaware   b. Virginia

   c. Colorado   d. Minnesota

7. One of these poisonous snakes is a member of the cobra family.

   a. rattlesnake   b. copperhead

   c. water moccasin   d. coral snake

8. Many recent and thrilling films have been made about one of these sea creatures.

   a. great white shark   b. sea bass

   c. moray eel   d. seal

Compare and Contrast

9. A friend and a relative.

10. Two different kinds of shoes.

Identify and Describe

11. William Jefferson Clinton

12. A famous actor or actress

13. **Explain** why you do or do not enjoy taking tests.

14. Only complete questions 2, 8, 9, 12, and 13.

MAKING AN OUTLINE

Making an outline, like narrowing a topic, that is, moving from the general to the specific, is not an easy task for students. Moving from the specific to the general is also hard, perhaps because school tasks are so often sequential. In the development of a narrative or an explanation of events, one moves chronologically from a *first*, to a *second*, and a *next*, until a *finally* is reached. Deductive and inductive thinking involve scale and proportion. In an auto repair course, a group of students might be given a large engine (generalization) to tear down into smaller parts (particulars) in order to find out how it works (deductive thinking). Another group of students might then be given the opportunity to scrutinize the parts and try to reconstruct the engine (inductive thinking). You can improve thinking skills, as many teachers do, by presenting daily exercises in deductive and inductive thinking in all courses. For example, in social studies class, use Socratic dialogue to challenge the assumptions of students about a particular social issue by asking questions and using analogies designed to make students rethink and clarify their positions. Hold mock "court" sessions in social studies and English classes, in which students gather evidence and argue persuasively for their positions. Both activities will help students maintain flexible attitudes when confronting social issues and/or personal problems later in life (Joyce et al. 1992).

Students with language difficulties are often passive thinkers. They have little confidence in their problem-solving capability, rarely ask questions, and let others do their thinking for them, thereby avoiding decisions and goal setting. Asking questions about the author's purpose before beginning a reading selection, during the reading to sustain interest, and after the reading to test for comprehension, stimulates critical thinking (Laskey and Gibson 1997). Alice Ansara (1966) believed that a reading teacher must be the "thinking" teacher, and that "thoughtful reading leads to a sharpening of perception, memory association, inductive thinking and concept formation.

Remind students that a broad topic or category can be likened to a wide fishing net, capable of catching all sorts of fish, whereas a smaller net may just catch a particular kind of fish. Point out that writing full of generalizations is boring and that specific details keep the reader's interest. Give students phrases orally such as "a great dinner," and have them describe hot seafood gumbo, spinach salad with black olives and feta cheese, and creamy Chicken Divan. Give them general topics such as *dogs, vacations,* or *Shakespeare* and have them make each topic more specific: *dachshunds, seashore,* and *Midsummer Night's Dream.* Give them statements to put in order.

Mr. Hyde was impulsive and had explosive tantrums.

Dr. Jekyll and Mr. Hyde had different personalities.

Dr Jekyll was a gentle man who read books of piety.

After students are proficient in these exercises, ask them to select a topic, narrow it, write a topic sentence (see Chapter 9), and make an outline before they write essays.

When it is time for students to tell what topics they have chosen, perhaps one of these students, a fifteen-year-old girl named Rhonda, looks disconsolate. Instead of answering, she shakes her head. When asked what is wrong, Rhonda says that she had chosen "vacation," as a topic, but that she just cannot write about it. Fortunately, the class is sympathetic and after more questions, the class discovers that Rhonda has been invited to Kenya to visit a friend in a few months. She cannot write about the subject because she feels "paralyzed" with fears. Her classmates ask her to explain why she is afraid, and she begins to talk about her various fears. The teacher lists them on the blackboard.

1) She has to get a passport, and doesn't know how.

2) She has to get shots for malaria and other diseases.

3) She has to buy luggage and a hat for a safari.

4) She is reluctant to leave her boyfriend, her friends, and her parents.

5) She wonders if something will happen to her on the safari.

6) She also has fears about being in a strange land, and around people who may not speak English.

After telling the class about her fears, Rhonda begins to feel better. The teacher tells Rhonda that writing about her fears may help her to take action and feel less threatened. With the help of the other students, the teacher makes an outline for Rhonda, but first Rhonda is asked why she wants to go to Kenya. Rhonda knowingly states that it will be the biggest adventure in her life.

Anticipating a great adventure—a trip to Kenya

I. Struggling with fears

   A. Fears about preparing for the trip

      1. Getting a passport

  2. Getting shots

  3. Having to buy luggage and a hat for safari

 B. Fears about leaving home

  1. Missing friends

  2. Missing boyfriend

  3. Missing parents

 C. Fears of being in a strange land

  1. No English-speaking people

  2. Having only one friend there

  3. Accident while on safari

II. Overcoming fears

 A. Taking action to overcome fears of getting ready for the trip

  1. Finding out how to get passport

  2. Making an appointment to get shots

  3. Going with friends to buy luggage and hat

 B. Overcoming fears of leaving people

  1. Having friends send letters

  2. Having boyfriend send several letters

  3. Calling parents long distance from Kenya

 C. Overcoming fears being in strange land

  1. Reading about people and culture

  2. Watching movies about safaris

  3. Realizing her friend will be a constant companion

As Rhonda has learned, making an outline is useful for setting priorities and solving problems, and is, therefore, a practical life skill, not merely an adjunct to writing papers.

Outlines are usually arranged in *chronological* order (sequential order), *numerical* order (size or number), *alphabetical* order (arranged in order from A to Z), and *place* order (according to location). There are five rules for correct outlining.

1) Title at the beginning.

2) Roman numerals to denote main topics.

3) Subtopics in descending order by capital letters, Arabic numerals, small letters in parentheses followed by small numerals in parentheses.

4) Subtopics indented to the right of the main topic, and divisions of subtopics indented to the right of subtopics. All topics of equal rank are in the same column.

5) Always two or more subtopics (Armstrong and Lampe 1983).

Although making an outline may seem an arduous and unnecessary task, it encourages clear thinking, logical sequence of ideas, and the ability to remember what has been learned. When writing essays and research papers, students will discover that outlining makes orderly writing possible.

USING THE LIBRARY

Teaching students how to use the library is often neglected. Although English teachers usually sign up their classes for brief tours of the library each year, students who are absent, in the Resource Room, or elsewhere in the building, might miss this overview of the library. Librarians, themselves, having become multi-media experts, are constantly helping and monitoring large groups of students using computers, checking out books, and passing in and out. Consequently, they rarely have extra time for educating students on the resources of the library. It is presumed that students already have learned these skills before entering high school. Moreover, a growing reliance on the computer as a reference center, where students are assisted in finding books, doing research, and exploring topics, has made some teachers deem it more important to teach students computer skills than how to find materials in a library. Nevertheless, the library remains a vital resource and students need to know that there is a system, that books are not randomly placed, and how and where to find the necessary books, magazines, or newspapers.

In many schools, card catalogs have become computerized, but students still need to know the meaning of call numbers and the importance of author, title, and subject. There are generally two systems of arranging books: The Library of Congress System and The Dewey Decimal System. The Dewey Decimal System is more common in school libraries, so students will need to know this system and the location of the divisions of books in a school or public library. How are fiction and nonfiction arranged? Where is the reference section, and what books are available there? Where are the magazines and newspapers?

Biography and fiction are most often set aside in a section arranged for both. Although some libraries classify individual biographies under 921, biography is generally classified by the number 92 or the letter *B*. Fiction is usually classified under *F* or *FIC* and arranged alphabetically by the authors' last name. The Dewey Decimal System is composed of ten divisions.

numbers	main divisions	subdivisions
000-099	General Works	encyclopedias, almanacs, bibliographies, magazines, newspapers.
100-199	Philosophy	Logic, philosophy, ethics, mythology, psychology.
200-299	Religion	Sacred writings, mythology, theologies.
300-399	Social Sciences	Communication, law, government, education, economics.
400-499	Language	Dictionaries, grammars, and technical studies of languages.

500-599	Science	Astronomy, biology, chemistry, physics.
600-699	Technology	Aviation, engineering, business, home economics, medicine.
700-799	Fine Arts	Architecture, music, painting, crafts, sports.
800-899	Literature	Literature, plays, essays, novels, poetry,
900-999	History	History, biography, geography.

Learning how to find books in the library can begin in the classroom. Give each student a copy of the Dewey Decimal System, and direct him or her to find the call numbers used for books on architecture, biology, medicine, philosophy or history. There will inevitably be a discussion of vocabulary. Students may have to find the definitions for words such as *philology, botany, mythology,* and *philosophy.* Many may not know the meaning of the words *fiction* and *nonfiction, biography, drama,* and *literature.*

There are four main sources of information in a library: reference books, magazines and newspapers, nonfiction and novels, and the computer. What would students expect to find in the reference section? For what reasons would students use the reference section? What kinds of information are available in various sets of encyclopedias, dictionaries, books with biographical information about famous authors, almanacs, and other important reference books? After further discussion on where to find books in the library, take students to the library for a tour, and show them where various kinds of books are found. Present them with a list of information to find in the library.

Because the card catalog has been computerized in many schools, students will need to know how to find the author, title, and call number of a book on the computer, as well as the variety of resources available on the Internet. Students must know how to conduct a key search on the Internet, which again involves narrowing or limiting a topic to find specific information.

There are an increasing number of resources in a library, and it is imperative that all students know, in general, where books are located, how to gain access to information using computers, and how to use card catalogs in locating books. Alice Ansara believed that when students understand the "language" of the library, they are able to ask knowledgeable questions about the materials they are seeking, and to use their time efficiently (1966).

FINDING BOOKS IN THE LIBRARY

List the call number, author, and title for the following books:

1. Any work of fiction _____

2. A biography _____

3. A book of poetry _____

4. A book about handicrafts _____

5. A book about philosophy _____

6. A book about fish _____

7. A book about American architecture _____

8. A dictionary _____

9. A magazine published in 1990 _____

10. A cookbook _____

11. A particular set of encyclopedias (include date)
_____

12. A book about agriculture _____

13. An almanac _____

14. A book about sociology _____

15. A book about eastern religions _____

16. A book about dance _____

17. The titles of two current periodicals _____

18. The name of two newspapers in the periodical room
_____

19. A book about China _____

20. A book of drama (plays) _____

21. A book about psychology _____

WRITING A RESEARCH PAPER

For students who intend to go to college, learning how to write research papers is essential. Alice Ansara thought few high school students understand the purpose of writing a research paper. More than being just another learning task, writing a research paper is a means of investigation ("developing inquiry of mind"). It stimulates original ideas and offers a method of gathering evidence to support these ideas (Ansara 1966).

Knowing where to find information in a library is a main concern. Before students begin their search for reading materials, be certain that they know where reference books are located and how to use the card catalog or the computer for locating books. If possible, individually guide students to the sections of the library important for their investigations.

Once students know how and where to find information, they should be encouraged to select topics that interest them. To choose topics randomly without wanting to know more about them is a mistake that will make drudgery out of inquiry. Ordinarily, students are given broad topics for consideration. In English class, they may be asked, for example, to write about the life of a contemporary author or to explore the current meaning of tragedy. In history, they may be asked to write about the Great Depression or World War I, and in science, students may be asked to research a single phenomenon of climate. The expectations, the language, and the format for the research paper may differ for each course.

Before choosing a topic, students should browse through several books on a topic they think may interest them. If the paper is for science, students may scan five books about climate before they choose from among the topics that interest them—acid rain, the diminishing ozone layer, global warming, or tornadoes. One student had recently heard of the destruction wreaked by a tornado in a nearby town, and he decided that he would like to know more about tornadoes. He began his research with 4" by 6" notecards, and 3" by 5" cards for a bibliography. As he browsed through books on tornadoes, he realized that the topic of tornadoes is vast, and that he must narrow or limit it to fit the scope of a twelve- page research paper.

As he read, he considered writing about the wind velocity in tornadoes, areas that are tornado-prone, the weather that spawns tornadoes, but finally he decided to do research on what happens in the aftermath of a tornado. He thought about the following questions: What is the extent of the damage? How are the victims' lives affected? The student was excited about this idea and discussed his topic with the science teacher. The teacher encouraged the student and even suggested that he travel to the nearby town to interview some of the recent tornado victims.

The student had a topic, but he needed to know how to paraphrase on 4" by 6" cards what he read, how to document his sources, and how to write bibliographical entries (author, title, publishing company, place of publishing and the date) on his 3" by 5" cards. Besides the books he skimmed on his topic, the student found information in magazines and newspapers; he conducted interviews and copied photographs, graphs, and articles from the computer. He was, however, careful to paraphrase this information, and to document it according to the guidelines provided by the teacher.

The student developed a thesis or statement of purpose: "Having experienced intense psychological, emotional and physical trauma, the lives of people who have lived through a tornado will never be the same." He then constructed an outline with an introduction about the power and destruction of tornadoes, but the main subtopics had to do with the psychological, emotional, and physical trauma experienced by the people who have lived through tornadoes.

Because he was confused about documentation, he received assistance from the teacher, who read his rough draft, commented first on how well the student had developed his main idea, advised him on how to rewrite parts of it, and helped him with paragraph transitions. The student also had to arrange his references or bibliography at the end of the paper in alphabetical order. When he completed his paper, the teacher asked the student to evaluate his own paper based on criteria developed by the teacher and students.

Ansara noted that writing papers assists students in reading because both language skills involve structure and particularity. Having learned how to write an organized research paper, students recognize the thought, structure, and details in another author's writing. If the student is also able to evaluate his own writing, "writing and reading will be seen as expression of thought and emotion, of personal and social need" (Ansara 1966).

Thus, by giving adolescents with dyslexia the tools for study and research, as well as the requisite language skills, you, the teacher or tutor, will be giving them the freedom to become independent learners. But, as Alice Ansara insisted, in order to accomplish this goal, these students must first be regarded as unique and whole human beings, who can be persuaded that it is never too late to read.

References

Alley, J., and Dohan, E.B. 1976. *Paragraphing*. Woburn, MA: Curriculum Associates.

The American Heritage Dictionary. 1991. Boston: Houghton Miffin Company.

Anderson, K. G. 1997. Gender Bias and Special Education Referrals. *Annals of Dyslexia* 47:151–61.

Ansara, A. 1966. *A Guide to the Teaching of Reading for Teachers of the Disadvantaged*. Cambridge, MA: Educators Publishing Service.

Ansara, A. 1969. *Maturational Readiness for School Tasks*. Bulletin of The Orton Society 19:51–59.

Ansara, A. 1969. Some Thoughts on Testing. *The Independent School Bulletin* 29:29–32.

Ansara, A. 1971. *Specific Language Disability*. Cambridge, MA: Educators Publishing Service.

Ansara, A. 1972a. Remediation for Adolescents. Lecture prepared for Dr. Jeanne Chall's class at Harvard.

Ansara, A. 1972b. *Salvaging the College Potential of Dyslexic Adolescents*. Bulletin of The Orton Society 22:123–39.

Ansara, A. 1972c. Background Paper for Section on Adolescents. Part of a lecture?

Ansara, A. 1973. *The Language Therapist as a Basic Mathematics Tutor for Adolescents*. Bulletin of The Orton Society 23:119–139.

Ansara, A. 1977. Classnotes of Constance Dwyer Porter taken during a class taught by Alice Ansara at St. Joseph's College in West Hartford, CT.

Ansara, A. 1977. Letter addressed to Richard J. McKay.

Ansara, A. 1978. Developing reading comprehension in dyslexic adolescents—the next "stage." Paper presented at the Annual Conference of The Orton Dyslexia Society, November, 1978, Minneapolis.

Ansara, A. 1979. Learning disabled and gifted and talented children and adolescents: similarities and differences. Paper presented at a conference of the National Association of Independent Schools. Madison, CT.

Ansara, A. 1982. The Orton-Gillingham Approach to Remediation in Developmental Dyslexia. In *Reading Disorders: Varieties and Treatments*, eds. R. N. Malatesha and P. G. Aaron. New York: Academic Press.

Armstrong, T. 1994. *Multiple Intelligences in the Classroom*. Alexandria, VA: Association for Supervision and Curriculum Development.

Armstrong, W. H., and Lampe, M. W. 1983. *Study Tactics*. New York: Barron's Educational Series.

Atwell, N. 1987. *In the Middle: Writing, Reading and Learning with Adolescents*. Portsmouth, NH: Boynton/Cook Publishers.

Bode, C., ed. 1947. *A Portable Thoreau*. New York: The Viking Press.

Bruner, J., Goodnow, J. J., and Austin, G.A. 1977. *A Study of Thinking*. Huntington, NY: R. E. Krieger Publisher.

Cohen, S. (1998, March 8). Miles and Miles. *Sunday Advocate*, pp.1D, 5D.

Cox, A. R. 1967. *Structures and Techniques of Remedial Language Training*. Cambridge, MA: Educators Publishing Service.

Facts about Dyslexia. 1993. National Institute of Child Health and Human Development (NICHD), in cooperation with The Orton Dyslexia Society. Washington, D.C.

Gillingham, A., and Stillman, B. 1956. *Remedial Training for Children with Specific Disability in Reading, Spelling, and Penmanship*. Cambridge, MA: Educators Publishing Service.

Gottesman, R. L., Bennett, R. E., Nathan, R. S., and Kelly, M. S. 1996. Inner-City Adults with Severe Reading Difficulties. *Journal of Learning Disabilities* 29:569–688.

Haley-James, S., and Stewig, J. W. 1990. *Houghton Mifflin English*. Boston: Houghton Mifflin Company.

Jensen, E. 1982. *Student Success Secrets*. New York: Barron's Educational Series.

Joyce, B., and Weil, M. with B. Showers. 1992. *Models of Teaching*. Boston: Allyn and Bacon.

Laskey, M. L. and Gibson, P. W. 1997. *College Study Strategies: Thinking and Learning*. Boston: Allyn and Bacon.

Marler, P. R., ed. 1972. *The Marvels of Animal Behavior*. Washington, D.C.: National Geographical Society.

McArthur, T., ed. *The Oxford Companion to the English Language*. 1992. Oxford: Oxford University Press.

Millman, J., and Pauk, W. 1969. *How To Take Tests*. New York: McGraw Hill.

Orton, S. T. 1937. *Reading, Writing and Speech Problems in Children*. New York: W.W. Norton and Company.

Phipps, R. 1983. *The Successful Student's Handbook.* Seattle: University of Washington Press.

Pirie, J., and Pirie, A. 1976. *Thirty Lessons in Notetaking.* Woburn, MA: Curriculum Associates.

Richards, F. M., and Romine, J. S. 1963. *Word Mastery.* Dubuque, Iowa: Wm. C. Brown Company.

Rudd, J. 1962. *Word Attack Manual.* Cambridge, MA: Educators Publishing Service.

Shaywitz, S. E., Shaywitz, B. A., Fletcher, J. M., and Escobar, M. D. 1990. Prevalence of Reading Disabilities in Boys and Girls: Results of the Connecticut Study, *Journal of the American Medical Association* 264: 998–1001.

Steere, A., Peck, C. Z., and Kahn, L. 1971. *Solving Language Difficulties.* Cambridge, MA: Educators Publishing Service.

Steinbeck, J. 1937. *The Red Pony.* Toronto: Bantam Books.

Virship, A. 1997, Feb. 2. Surfing. *The Washington Post Magazine.* pp. 10–13, 24–30.

Warren, R. P. 1968. *Why Do We Read Fiction? The American Experience.* New York: The MacMillan Company.

Index